RUDYARD KIPLING
and his world

Rudyard Kipling

KINGSLEY AMIS

RUDYARD KIPLING
and his world

THAMES AND HUDSON
LONDON

Frontispiece: pencil drawing of
Kipling by William Strang, A R A
(1859–1921).

*Printed in Great Britain
by Jarrold and Sons Ltd, Norwich*

Kipling at Bateman's

The Philip Burne-Jones portrait of
Carrie Kipling.

He came here when he was thirty-six
And left for good thirty-four years later.
She organized his life, dealt with all his
Correspondence, set out his engagements,
Filtered his visitors, so that nothing
Could ever come between him and his work.

There's a portrait of her in the study:
Not bad, by Philip Burne-Jones, his cousin;
Less than full length, cut off near the ankles,
Supposedly to conceal her smallness;
Her look one of calm or satisfaction,
And, hanging from her waist, some sort of key.

In a work of this modest length, and with the field so thoroughly worked over in three-quarters of a century of Kipling studies, I have not been concerned to find and reveal new facts, though several unregarded ones have come my way. There are, I hope, some new interpretations, emphases and connections here, and the critical judgments are my own, which is not to say that they do not often agree with others'.

To spare the reader's patience, I have presented without qualification inferences which I have firm grounds for considering accurate, dropping wherever possible such biographer's lifebelts as 'perhaps', 'probably' and 'it may be assumed'; but when I am in doubt I say so. From similar motives, wherever possible I have dropped the quotation marks I might have hung round phrases not my own, those deriving from memoirs, letters, critical or biographical pieces, the works of the subject himself. Again, when I want to make it clear that I am reporting someone else's words I do so, providing the attribution where it seems desirable and useful. To give names and other details is so often to give profitless trouble: who, for instance, would be much better off for being told, in parenthesis or footnote, that it was Kipling's eldest aunt's granddaughter Angela Mackail, later the novelist Angela Thirkell, who described as 'deep and unhesitating' his voice when telling stories to children?

I am profoundly grateful to Professor Charles Carrington, without whose official biography, *Rudyard Kipling: his life and work*, this essay of mine could never have been contemplated. My debt to it is such that I must mention it here as well as in the Bibliography, which lists my main sources of information or critical enlightenment and may also help those who would like to find out more for themselves.

I am also greatly obliged to Thames and Hudson Ltd for commissioning me to write this text. If they had not done so, I might never have fully discovered the work of a great English writer.

January 1975   K.A.

PHYSICALLY, RUDYARD KIPLING WAS A SMALL MAN. Five foot six inches is the official estimate, though, in the later nineteenth century, this would not have been so very much below average height, and perhaps we should scale him down by an inch or two. He had some breadth of shoulder, striking some observers as thickset, others as slim. Until the end of his life, his bearing was upright and his movements quick and agile. His hands and feet matched his small stature. He never fumbled, and his gestures were always expressive.

His head, set on a short neck, was of unusual modelling, with a rather large, dark-complexioned face, a sharply receding forehead and a massive, strongly cleft chin. The partial loss of his dark-brown hair started in early manhood; he had a pair of broad black eyebrows and, in maturity, a heavy moustache that partly hid his mouth. From the age of eleven, he was compelled by extreme short sight to wear thick glasses at all times. Some of these characteristics might be thought to serve equally well an aggressive aspect and the concealment of emotion; in fact, his bright blue eyes had a thoughtful, sober look, and their direct glance was penetrating, humorous and warm.

In telling stories to children, a favourite activity, his voice was described as deep and unhesitating; on public occasions it was dignified, well modulated, and faintly sad in its cadence. His diction was clear, with an individual pronunciation of vowels. In conversa- tion he spoke rapidly, as befitted his vivacious, alert, communicative demeanour. He had plenty to say, but was also given to asking questions, and, what is much rarer, to listening to the answers, as so much of his work testifies. Although not a wit in the sense of a coiner of epigrams, he was a good anecdotalist, and his powers of repartee were famous.

Spy's cartoon was used as the frontispiece to Kipling's *The Art of Fiction*, 1926.

John Lockwood Kipling married
Alice Macdonald at St Mary
Abbot's old church, Kensington, in
1865.

Opposite, a suitably Indian subject
used by John Lockwood Kipling as
a book-plate for Rudyard.

The Kiplings were a Yorkshire family, perhaps derived ultimately
from Scandinavia. According to Kipling himself, they 'seem to have
included small farmers, bell-founders, clock-makers, and the like'.
Although he once called Yorkshire the best county in England, and
made one of his Soldiers Three (the least interesting of the three) a
Yorkshireman, Kipling took no step of any kind towards his
native heath when he settled in this country after half a lifetime spent
mostly abroad. Just the opposite might have been expected of a man
so deeply absorbed in the lives of the English people over the centuries.
But boredom with one's own ancestry need not run counter to any
of that, and may even be thought an amiable trait.

Kipling's father and mother are nearer our concern; they were
certainly very near his heart to the end of their days. John Lockwood
Kipling, born in 1837, was a craftsman and an artist, a sculptor, an
architect, an illustrator, a scholar and a capable writer: in due time,
the son professed to think the father a better stylist than himself.

EX LIBRIS

RUDYARD KIPLING

K

19
09

II

Bombay harbour. The town prospered during the 1860s, and even more so after the opening of the Suez Canal at the end of the decade.

Nobody has been found to share that view, but John came to be Rudyard's most valued critic, almost at times his collaborator. John's wife, *née* Alice Macdonald, was of Irish and Welsh as well as Scotch descent. Born in the same year as her husband, she was a cut or so above him socially. Three of her younger sisters married respectively the eminent painter Edward Burne-Jones, the then equally eminent though now-forgotten painter Edward Poynter, and a rich industrialist called Alfred Baldwin (the last match was to produce the

future Prime Minister, Stanley Baldwin). In comparison, John Kipling must have seemed like nobody in particular.

He and Alice were married in London on 18 March 1865. Within a month they had sailed for Bombay, where John was to take up a professional post in a newly founded art school. The appointment preceded, indeed made possible, the marriage, and according to contemporary rumour it had been secured through the influence of Alice's brother. She was a more forceful person than her husband,

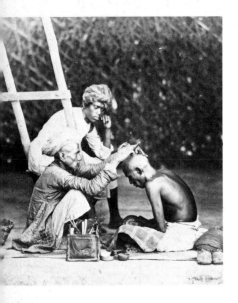

John Lockwood Kipling was a
careful – and imaginative – observer
of the Indian way of life. His
drawing of a barber (*above right*) and
the similar photograph (*above*) both
date from the early 1870s.

with a fluent and witty tongue that could turn to sharpness. It is
tempting to see her as the propelling power behind the move to India,
whether as a gesture of independence from her family or as a way of
withdrawing from competition with them. But there seems to be no
real evidence to support this interpretation, and quite as likely the
young couple between them found the prospect novel and exciting.
It was certainly a much more adventurous step than it might seem
to us today.

In 1865, 'India' of course comprised not only present-day India, but
also Pakistan, Bangladesh and the lower half or so of Burma. Although a good third of the territory consisted of Native States under
petty princes who retained some local powers, in practice the British
ran the whole sub-continent. The British Empire – used in many
contexts as a virtual synonym for 'India' – was nearly complete.
Upper Burma remained to be annexed in 1886.

There had been British on the scene, under the East India Company
('East India' was a vague area also comprising what was once the
Dutch East Indies and elsewhere), since the early seventeenth century.
The Company's troops, increasingly supplemented by British
regular forces under interim arrangements, had succeeded for many
years in maintaining some sort of control in a part of the world that
had known continual wars, invasions and massacres for centuries.
But in 1857 there came the Indian Mutiny, in fact a series of bloody
local revolts with some similarity (we need not discuss here how
important) to a war of independence. Order was restored, and the
Company's authority formally passed to the British Crown, in 1858;

Contemporary map of India, 1877.

The devastation of the Indian Mutiny was recorded by the camera of Felice Beato.

peace was proclaimed in the following year – less than six years before the arrival of the Kiplings.

Violence had ceased, but the threat of it – less against the British than between national, religious and tribal groups – would remain and, in not-so-distant dealings of the Empire, be made actual. Actual too were the regional famines and epidemics which the over-worked, understaffed authorities fought to alleviate. The India, the Empire, in which Rudyard Kipling was to do a large part of his growing-up should not be thought of as a more or less quiescent society under a benevolent (or rigid) despotism, much more as a ramshackle creation which might begin to fall apart, with results that needed no imagining, if a river-bridge were to be carried away in a flood, if a subaltern should panic, for want of a nail. Nobody on the spot could have seen the situation like that all the time; for most, there was a state of complacency touched now and again by fear.

Joseph Rudyard Kipling was born in Bombay, an important and thriving colonial city, on 30 December 1865. The first Christian name, that of his father's father, was never used, except presumably at his baptism in the Cathedral there; the second, often shortened to Ruddy, commemorated his parents' first meeting on a picnic at Lake Rudyard (now Rudyard Reservoir, near Leek, Staffordshire).

The custom of leaving largely to servants the upbringing of young children, standard among the Victorian upper classes, flourished in the Empire, the more so because of the cheapness of servant labour.

The Indian Punch was no less preoccupied with middle-class servant problems than its British counterpart, but there were at least some different faces in the drawing-room. Cartoon of 1863.

WHAT IMPUDENCE.

AMY.—"Oh, Gussy dear, what do you think that thing of an Ayah says?"
AUGUSTUS.—"What, dear?"
AMY.—"Why, that she has a daughter the very picture of me. Did you ever know such impudence?"

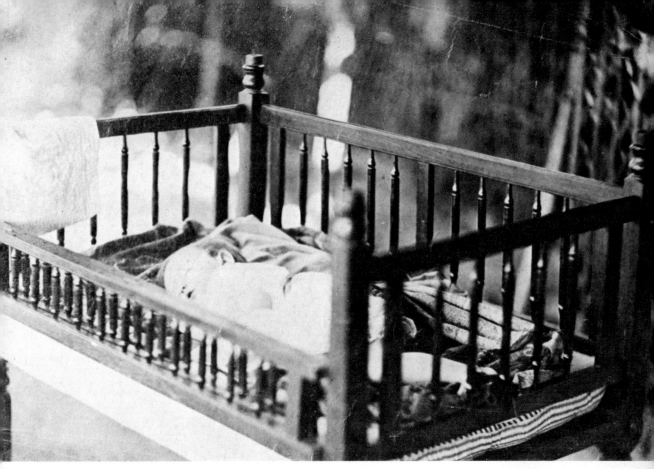

DOMESTIC OCCURRENCES.

[The charge for notifying a Domestic Occurrence is one Rupee.]

BOMBAY.

BIRTHS.

WADDINGTON—December 29th, at Poona, the wife of Captain T. Waddington, Educational Inspector, Central Division, of a son.

SMITH—December 30th, the wife of George Smith, Commander of ship *Oriflamme*, of a daughter.

KIPLING—December 30th, on the Esplanade, Bombay, the wife of J. Lockwood Kipling, Esq , of a son.

MADRAS.

BIRTHS.

FREDERICKS—On Christmas Eve, at Madras, the wife of Mr. J. H. Fredericks, of a daughter.

LIDDELL—December 26th, at Egmore, Madras, the wife of W. B. Liddell, Esq., of a son.

MARRIAGES.

DIXON—CHAMBERLAIN—December 11th, at Jubbulpore, by Rev. C. Cahusac, Capt. E. G. Dixon, 10th M. N. I., to Alice, eldest daughter of Charles Chamberlain, Esq., Gloucester House, Malvern Wells, Worcestershire.

CALENDAR—JANUARY 1866.

Above, the infant Rudyard in his cot.

Left, *The Times of India* records his birth for a fee of one rupee.

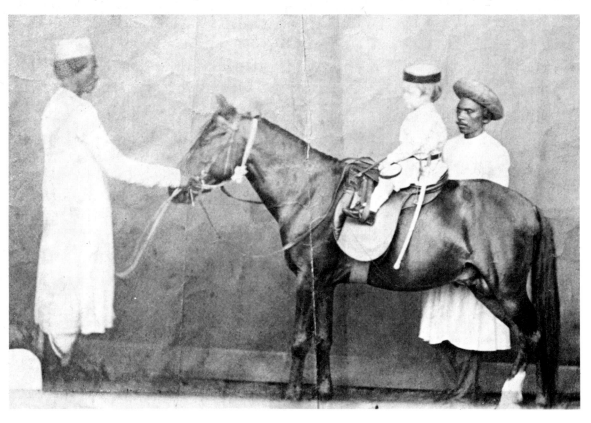

The young Rudyard in the saddle,
ministered to by his servants.

The infant Rudyard had at his beck and call an *ayah* or nanny, the
Hindu bearer who attended his father, and any or every other domestic
within range. He was an unquestioned despot; when, in an early
story, he wrote of a six-year-old boy, 'it never entered his head that
any living human being [even Papa and Mama?] could disobey his
orders', he clearly had in mind himself at that age.

Such unwelcome notions did more than enter the head of the
two-and-a-bit-year-old Rudyard when his mother took him back to
England with her to await the birth of her second child. Her parents
found him difficult at best; her sister Louisa Baldwin noted that he
was highly strung and ill ordered, given to screaming tempers when
crossed. Unquestioned despotism was restored as soon as the party,
now augmented by one, arrived back in Bombay. The addition was
the newborn Alice Kipling, always to be known as Trix. The two
children continued in India for nearly another three years.

It is clear that young Rudyard was as thoroughly spoilt as most
boys could hope to be. But that spoiling must be understood only in
its weaker sense of over-indulgence. No adverse mark was left on his
character. When he grew up, he showed no more – perhaps even
rather less – exasperation at resistance to his wishes than the average

man. He was never an egotist. So far from taking amiss the advent of a younger sister as a threat to his supremacy, he at once conceived a devotion to her that was to last all his life. The circumstances of his early childhood in fact were uniquely valuable in his growth as a writer; without them, he would have been not only different but diminished.

Being cosseted by native servants meant affection and intimacy, and that intimacy meant, above all, that he learned their language, Hindustani or 'the vernacular', actually a form of Hindi with a large admixture of Arabic, Persian and other foreign elements. It was so much his language that he thought and dreamed in it, and had to be prompted to speak English with his parents as best he could. When, at the age of sixteen, he returned to India from England, he was to

'Ruddy's idea of heaven' as a child of two, a drawing by his indulgent but amiably sardonic father.

Bombay: 'a blazing beauty of a city', according to John Lockwood Kipling. It was the richly Indian atmosphere, rather than the 'beauty' of such places as the cotton ground (*above*) and Borah Bazaar (*above right*) that was to influence his son.

find himself making remarks in the vernacular of which he did not know the meaning – if literally true, an unexpected lift for the behaviourist school of linguistics.

With this key, Kipling had access to an India never approachable by most Europeans. He was also free to go where no adult of his race could venture, as into Hindu temples, and would be taken where few such adults would care to go, as to the food-market and perhaps to less salubrious quarters. All those colours and sounds and smells made an impression on him that was distinctive as well as deep: a child born among them would no doubt find them wonderful, but he would not find them strange, would apprehend them the more clearly for having no preconceptions.

Not every Anglo-Indian* child grew into a writer of genius. Kipling of course brought qualities of his own to these early experiences: a truly insatiable curiosity, prodigious powers of observation and a staggering memory: an elderly Parsee testified in 1936 that the five-year-old Kipling never forgot a face or a name, and the grown-up Kipling took no notes of what he saw and heard. The happy combination of qualities and experiences conclusively shaped his development. He himself, unsurprisingly, had the insight to acknowledge the enduring power upon him of that extraordinary time. At the start of *Something of Myself*, the autobiographical work he drafted in his last months, he applies to his own case the Jesuit motto, 'Give me the first six years of a child's life and you can have the rest.' At least three of his stories include a more or less direct portrayal of his Indian childhood, but its reverberations can be felt on every page he wrote about India.

* In those days an Anglo-Indian was a person of British birth living in India.

He was not yet six when his existence suffered a violent change. The common contemporary practice of sending children away from home to be educated was reinforced among the Anglo-Indians by the understandable desire to remove their young from an environment so conducive to deadly disease: Alice herself lost a newborn second son in 1870. In the spring of 1871, all four Kiplings left Bombay for England; in the December of that year, Rudyard and Trix were boarded out with foster-parents at Southsea near Portsmouth.

The wisdom of the move in itself can hardly be debated today. What has aroused some continuing puzzlement is the parents' choice of foster-home. Five households of relatives might be thought to have been available: the senior Kiplings', the senior Macdonalds', the Burne-Joneses', the Poynters' and the Baldwins'. The last three had young children of their own, and Rudyard was particularly attached to his Aunt Georgiana (Burne-Jones). John and Alice chose to board their offspring with a couple called Holloway, known to them only from a newspaper advertisement and – no doubt satis-factory – references. More surprisingly still, the parents made no adequate attempt to explain what was afoot, leaving Rudyard and Trix to discover for themselves that they were now living with a pair of strangers known as Uncle Harry and Aunty Rosa.

This – the failure to warn – was certainly unkind, though it might well have been the product less of callousness than of defective imagination, or of a faint-hearted but surely not inexplicable reluctance to face the storm of fury which Rudyard was bound to have raised, given the chance. Various half-excuses have been proffered for the decision to put the children into the care of outsiders: such an arrangement was not as uncommon then as it would be today; there would be frequent alleviating visits to and from relatives; Alice Kipling's desire for independence was again at work. I think it was largely a matter of saving trouble. Grandparents, uncles and aunts (especially aunts) would complain, criticize, send bothersome reports of Ruddy's tantrums, expect gratitude, excuses, etc.; the Holloways were being paid to do a job.

Saving trouble is not in itself to be reprehended, and if things had gone at all well at Lorne Lodge, that cramped, chilly dwelling, not much in the way of explanation or extenuation would have been called for. As it was, things seemed to go notoriously badly. Captain Holloway – the rank refers to the merchant marine, or was a courtesy title – showed some friendliness to young Rudyard, but died before half the boy's stay in the household was over. Thereafter, Aunty Rosa tyrannized over him, willingly abetted by her adolescent son. There were regular inquisitions and beatings, often with a pseudo-religious excuse. In time, there was an unpleasant, plebeian day-

Rudyard aged six, when he went to the 'House of Desolation', Lorne Lodge.

Lorne Lodge, 'smelling of aridity and emptiness', and leaving a very different impression from his Indian experience.

school. To make matters worse, Trix was taken into extravagant favour by the family. Life was hell in all its terrors. No wonder that, when Alice Kipling, informed from different sources that her son's sight was failing and his morale low, returned to Southsea and came up to his bedroom to kiss him good night, he flung up an arm to guard off the blow that he had been trained to expect.

So runs the account, and much of it must be true. Some writers have swallowed it whole and used it to support theories of irreversible psychological damage issuing in a lifelong proneness to revenge-fantasies, or something like that. Others have rightly been more cautious. The foundations on which the account rests, though tangible, are all shaky. In 1888, Kipling published the longish short story, 'Baa, Baa, Black Sheep', in which the persecutions outlined above are rehearsed in detail and with an air of great bitterness. But it is a *story*: the author is not on oath; he must be expected, like

Rudyard was able to escape from Southsea and to stay at the Grange in Fulham during holidays. There – at the home of Aunt Georgie and Uncle Ned Burne-Jones – he was able to play with the Burne-Jones children, and also with those of Uncle Topsy (William Morris). *Left to right*, Margaret Burne-Jones, May Morris, Jenny Morris, Philip Burne-Jones.

other authors, to have heightened such real experiences as might befall him by selective emphasis and even more by omission. Black Sheep, the Rudyard character, is never let out of his hell until the final rescue by his mother. We know that this was far from true of the real Rudyard. The picture of school life is self-evidently lopsided.

Kipling returned to the theme two years later in the first chapter of his first novel, *The Light that Failed*. Here, there are again persecutions and beatings, but no figures corresponding to the Captain or the Holloway son, and the hero and his young girl companion are held in equal disesteem by the Aunty Rosa character. Once again, this is fiction, though it might well be argued by some that the 'Southsea' episode significantly fails to be an altogether appropriate prelude to the later events of the novel.

Finally, there are two avowedly autobiographical accounts of those years. One is to be found in *Something of Myself*. This is a fascinating book, but Kipling did not live to revise it, and other parts of it are provenly inaccurate. It would be difficult to refute the view that the aged author was drawing upon memories not so much of fact as of 'Baa, Baa, Black Sheep'. The same might be said of the fourth source, an essay by Trix, also composed late in life. Her expressed feeling that the story somewhat exaggerated the real situation at Lorne Lodge is quite compatible with her having none the less drawn upon it unconsciously, and is interesting too.

We should also note, or remember, that when Louisa Baldwin visited her nephew and niece in 1872 she found them seemingly very well and happy, and Mrs Holloway 'a very nice woman indeed'; that Rudyard on arrival had had an almost continuous record of unquestioned despotism; and that most children, especially perhaps those brought up in an environment in which class and caste are noticeable, suffer from acute snobbery. Whatever her virtues or vices, Aunty Rosa was no *memsahib*, and any old tantrum might have been expected to bring up that fact. In particular, when Rudyard had been removed from her authority, Trix was allowed to stay with her on and off for three more years. As several commentators have noticed, this renders the upflung-arm incident (featured in *Something of Myself* as well as in 'Baa, Baa, Black Sheep') suspect in the extreme. It would have taken a much harder woman than Alice Kipling to ignore such plain evidence of cruelty.

The foregoing paragraphs are not intended to suggest that Rudyard's life at Southsea was ruffled only by minor inconveniences. On any reading of the matter, he suffered a great deal, but just how much, in just what ways, and out of just what mixture of firmness and brutality are questions we are not likely to see answered. It is far easier to estimate the effect of those years on his character. All children, unquestioned despots or not, need opposition at some stage before puberty, and whereas a big stick and a couple of hell-fire specialists are not the ideal instruments to provide it, Rudyard got what he needed. He may have got other things besides: the themes of betrayal, ill-treatment and revenge do run through his work, though he is quite as likely to have acquired these interests at his public school; his attitude to women is sometimes unfavourable, though this could be said of plenty of men with no Aunty Rosa in their early lives. He himself asserted, perhaps sardonically, that it was all good training for a writer: close observation of moods, of how words and actions diverged, and so on.

The only certain result of these experiences that was certainly bad is 'Baa, Baa, Black Sheep'. It is a sorry tale in all senses, devoid of any conflict or tension, with a stated moral but no real point, and damagingly silent about the motives of Aunty Rosa – the character is given the same name as the person. Black Sheep might well have been unable to understand them, but even a far less skilful writer could have found a way to fill that vacuum. As it is, the story lacks all balance. Trix said Kipling wrote it in a towering rage, not an advantageous state of mind in which to set about producing art.

On the positive side, it may well be that Kipling's attitude to children, with its special tenderness and understanding, was partly derived from the memory of his own unhappiness. He clearly thought so. And, far from growing into a timid, insecure man, he proved notably self-reliant, undertaking long solitary journeys across India from the age of nineteen. He matured decidedly early in all ways, having, so to speak, got his childhood over in one go, short and sharp. Whatever evil he endured, some good came out of it.

Finally, it might be noted that, between beatings, he had found time to read a fair amount – not only *Robinson Crusoe*, Hans Andersen, *Little Women*, but also Bunyan, Fielding, Dickens – and that his unpleasant day-school, which provided among other things a naval education, had not only grounded him in Latin and mathematics, but sent him away with the temporary ambition of joining the Royal Navy. That could never have happened to Black Sheep.

Alice Kipling removed Rudyard from the 'House of Desolation' in March 1877. They and Trix spent the summer on a farm in Epping Forest. Here there was a great deal of outdoor activity and, glasses having now been provided, a great deal of reading on Rudyard's part. This continued through the autumn, when the trio stayed in lodgings in Brompton Road, then a relatively remote corner of London. He and Trix were given season tickets for the Victoria and Albert Museum, and used them to the full. Congenitally fascinated by objects, he took everything in, from what held no relevance to his later interests – musical instruments – to what held a great deal –

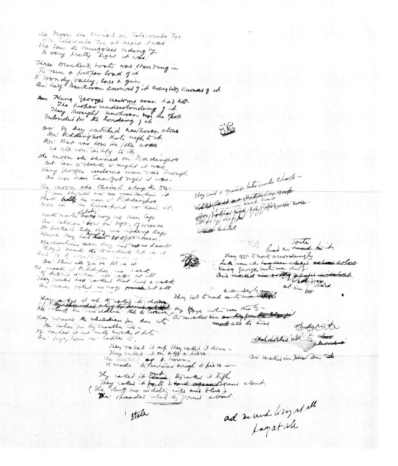

Rudyard found the scientific instruments, and the manuscripts, in the Victoria and Albert Museum irresistible. *Above*, a sixteenth-century astronomical globe incorporating a clock, from the Museum. *Above right*, the heavy revisions – if not so much the subject-matter – of the last page Dickens wrote, from *Edwin Drood*, are matched (*right*) by a manuscript of a Kipling poem.

mechanical models. Above all, there was the manuscript of a Dickens novel, full of revisions. By now, rising twelve, the young Kipling not only understood that 'books and pictures were among the most important things in the world'; he had himself started to write.

By his own account, it was during the couple of months in Brompton Road that Kipling first suffered from the insomnia that stayed with him all his life. 'The night got into my head,' as he put it, and he would go and wander through the house and round the garden. Such nocturnal rambles became a habit for many years. A poem of the 1890s clearly refers to himself: 'We wakeful; oh, pity us!' Pity is probably due, but readers of Kipling will accord it with mixed feelings. They have benefited from what he suffered: places, like objects, are an important part of his subject-matter, and nobody knows a place intimately until he has known it at night.

The happy interlude ended. Rudyard was to be sent to school in earnest. His luck held, in the sense that his early life continued to be quite different from that of any other writer; in the ordinary sense, his luck was out again, at any rate to begin with. He had wanted to go to Harrow like his cousin Stanley Baldwin; where he went was to a recently founded establishment, the United Services College at Westward Ho!, a north Devon seaside resort that had failed to make its way. The buildings, a terrace block run into one, were unprepossessing; the food was barely adequate; discipline was severe,

Stanley Baldwin, aged nine.

Kipling's school, founded in 1874 by a group of retired Army officers who could not afford the fees at established schools.

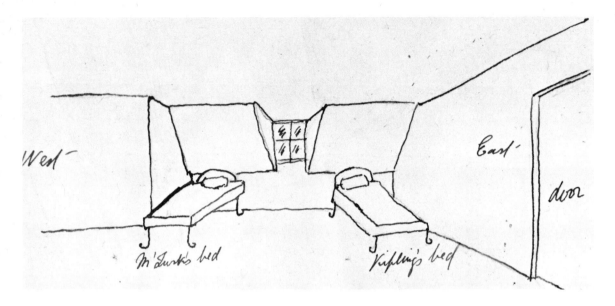

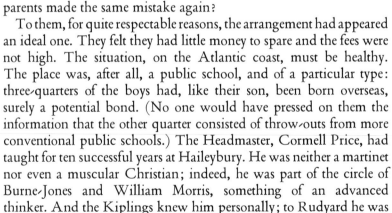

G. C. Beresford (M'Turk) presented an appropriately austere view of the curtainless dormitory in which he slept with Kipling.

Cormell Price.

especially in the hands of the cane-wielding Chaplain; there were bullies among the boys, as Rudyard repeatedly discovered during his first year or more. It was Southsea on a larger scale. Had the parents made the same mistake again?

To them, for quite respectable reasons, the arrangement had appeared an ideal one. They felt they had little money to spare and the fees were not high. The situation, on the Atlantic coast, must be healthy. The place was, after all, a public school, and of a particular type: three-quarters of the boys had, like their son, been born overseas, surely a potential bond. (No one would have pressed on them the information that the other quarter consisted of throw-outs from more conventional public schools.) The Headmaster, Cormell Price, had taught for ten successful years at Haileybury. He was neither a martinet nor even a muscular Christian; indeed, he was part of the circle of Burne-Jones and William Morris, something of an advanced thinker. And the Kiplings knew him personally; to Rudyard he was already 'Uncle Crom'; he would escort the lad down from London on his first day.

Price undoubtedly had some excellent qualities, but if he had only been a little less of an advanced thinker and a little more of a martinet, he might have treated as urgent the task of introducing a measure of order into his school, curbed the Chaplain, looked out for bullies and punished them. (There is good independent testimony that Kipling's recollections of his first year at the College are trustworthy.) As it was, life was 'brutal'. Rudyard wrote to his mother – who was still in England: she stayed for nearly two more years – and told her so, something he had never done at Southsea. She was distressed, and complained mildly to Price, but took no further action. When, at the end of Rudyard's first term, the Easter holidays came, so far from allowing him to spend them with her, she went to Italy to join her husband, then on his way home from India. Nor were arrangements made for the boy to visit relatives: he had to stay on at school. To devise a charitable explanation for this behaviour on Alice's part is difficult, but there may just conceivably be some extenuating facts of which we know nothing.

In time, things at the College began to improve as the place settled down. The cane-wielding Chaplain was replaced by a pipe-smoking muscular Christian. The bullying died away, or at any rate ceased to involve the growing Rudyard. He formed a close alliance with two other boys; they came to share a study which they decorated themselves after a mildly Bohemian fashion. The trio went in for rule-breaking escapades, equally mild by today's standards and rather ordinary by any, though not such as to endear them to authority. Their position as the school intellectuals was at least tolerated.

School was not all privation and unhappiness, as Rudyard's letter of 9 March 1882 indicates.

Rudyard emerged as the school writer, contributing a large part of the contents of its magazine, becoming secretary of its literary society, composing verses for its yearly concert. He remained on good terms with his Headmaster and acquired the friendship of one or two others. He was fitting in. The only school activity in which, because of his short sight, he could not join was organized games, and that only meant more time for reading.

Also ruled out in this way was any kind of career in the Army, for which most of the other pupils were destined and the College curriculum designed. Apart from a training in Latin and study of the Third Book of Horace's *Odes*, Kipling's formal education included English, French, and mathematics (at which he was a dud). It seems clear, however, and unsurprising, that the general approach was utilitarian, much more so than that prevailing in the conventional schools of the era. In an article written some years later, Kipling praised the College for turning out 'men who do real work' as opposed to men who merely write about the doing of that real work (an excellent summary of his own distinction as a writer), and added the following sneer:

A scholar may, as the Latin masters said, get more pleasure out of his life than an Army officer, but only little children believe that a man's life is given him to decorate with pretty little things, as though it were a girl's room or a picture screen [or a school study?].

Anyone who really thinks that the works of Virgil or Catullus (or Horace) are pretty little things, or that all they can do is decorate a man's life, has not been properly educated. Perhaps Kipling did not really think so; perhaps, in that passage, he was crying sour grapes. Nevertheless, his education was not proper, not suitable in two important ways.

Intimate knowledge of a foreign – preferably classical – language and some representative part of its literature, such as Kipling never attained, is an important part of a writer's training. Thereafter he will use words with a heightened feeling for their appropriateness to any given context; he will have acquired linguistic perspective. What can they know of English who only English know? That would be to overstate Kipling's position: he became devoted to Horace, he 'knew' Hindustani, though in a quite non-literary way, he learned to read French, and a great sensitivity to words was obviously born in him. But that sensitivity can be seen, here and there in his works, to have remained to some extent uncultivated; he will obtrude his attention to matters of style and treatment (forgetting the Horatian slogan to the effect that technique should be invisible), or, less often, he will be insufficiently attentive.

Q. HORATI FLACCI

CARMINUM LIBRUM

QUINTUM

A

RUDYARDO KIPLING

ET

CAROLO GRAVES

ANGLICE REDDITUM

ET VARIORUM NOTIS ADORNATUM
AD FIDEM CODICUM MSS. EDIDIT
ALUREDUS D. GODLEY

Editio Altera

OXONII
APUD BASILIUM BLACKWELL
MDCCCCXX

Kipling's grounding in Horace at school provided him with a life-long interest.

Kipling suffered in another and more material sense from the deficiencies of the teaching at the College. It not only deprived him, it ordered matters so that he remained deprived. A course of study at Oxford or Cambridge would have put things right, but both roads to it were closed. There was presumably not enough parental money to buy a place, and the College entirely lacked the elaborate machinery required to train candidates for scholarships. To his own keen regret, Kipling's formal education ended early, when he was not much over sixteen and a half.

Self-education via private reading is not really education at all, but it may help a developing writer to find his feet. Rudyard had arrived at Westward Ho! well acquainted with many of the English classics. In time, he and his two cronies came to share an enthusiasm for Ruskin, Carlyle and Browning, not the most obvious authors to attract it from schoolboys. Cormell Price gave him the run of his library. Rudyard worked his way through the poets from Donne to Swinburne, was significantly captivated by Peacock and his practice of scattering poems among his tales, discovered Russian writers in French translation. His fondness for American authors – Emerson, Longfellow, Poe, Whitman, Bret Harte, Mark Twain – was unusual in the England of his day.

None of all this, nor his own habitual verse-writing, would have gone down very well at the orthodox Victorian public school. The College, however, was in certain respects a remarkably easy-going institution. It existed to get boys into the Army, not to build their characters. Prowess at games was not set above intellectual ability; Rudyard himself, already a personality of some power, may have done something to encourage this tendency. Something called the United Services College might have been expected to be sharply military in practice and ethos; in fact, bugle-calls, both literal and metaphorical, were altogether absent. To see the place as any kind of forcing-ground for imperialists would be false.

Neither was it any sort of annexe to the Church. Price was rather exceptional among Victorian headmasters in not being a clergyman nor even a dedicated Christian – an added recommendation from the point of view of John and Alice Kipling, themselves no church-goers. The College had a Chaplain but no chapel, and after the cane-wielder's departure that Chaplain was far more likely to offer Rudyard (in his last year, at any rate) tobacco and whisky than spiritual guidance. No encouragement was given to any of the religious enthusiasms common at the time. Perhaps Kipling would never have been touched by them; he became, at any rate, a man of no strong faith, for whom the Christian God's chief importance was as a figure to be invoked when some more immediate concern called for support or opposition.

William Morris (*right*) and Edward
Burne-Jones in the garden at the
Grange.

Other beliefs, of more moment to him, were reinforced or acquired
at the College. His own reading, allied with holiday visits to the
Burne-Joneses and the Poynters, had convinced him that art – 'books
and pictures' – was nearly all-important. The only other thing that
counted was the path of action, the 'real work' that was waiting to
be done by his schoolfellows when they entered upon their careers.
Most young men – for Rudyard was a man at sixteen – would have
seen a conflict here, a clash between the life of art, of Burne-Jones's
languid pictures, of Morris's mock-medieval ballads, and the life
of Army and Empire. Kipling never saw it like that. He questioned
neither and accepted both: he would use his art to celebrate work.
Without the need for those spectacles of his, he might have combined

the two differently, becoming an English de Vigny or an English Lermontov. I would rather have what we have.

There is some sort of account of Kipling's schooldays in his *Stalky & Co.*, published in 1899, but we must be careful in determining what sort. Some parts of it can be accepted as factual: the buildings, the setting, the routine, the hut in the furze-bushes used as a refuge from discipline, the decorated study where prep was shared out, the obsessive reading, the minor infractions of rules. Beyond such matters, fiction keeps breaking in. The three central characters are usually taken as portraits – 'Beetle' founded on Kipling himself, 'Stalky' and 'M'Turk' on Kipling's two associates. 'Portrait' and 'founded on'

Kipling as a schoolboy in 1882; his short sight gave him the nickname 'Gigger' (from the slang for spectacles, 'Giglamps') and excused him from at least some games.

The formidable threesome in *Stalky & Co.*

are difficult expressions; so too, in Kipling's statement that he and the others were the 'originals' of the three, is 'originals'. Even the most conscientiously literal account of real people or incidents must be distorted by selection and emphasis, and Kipling was writing tales, and the tales have plots, and plots have a way of shaping character to suit themselves. Other figures in the book, notably the masters, cannot be claimed to be more than 'loosely based on' real people, and the central incidents – the circumventions of authority, the elaborate ruses, the ingenious table-turnings – are demonstrably made up. This would not be worth saying if the book had not so often been mistaken for a lightly edited record of what 'really' went on at the College.

Fiction can be autobiographical in a secondary sense, can be taken as a record, if not of what the writer experienced, at any rate of what he felt and thought in the process of creation. Seen in this way, *Stalky & Co.* has been made to support the view that Kipling was still, after more than fifteen years, smarting at the cruel and unfair treatment he had received at the College, so much so that he decided to pay back his persecutors with even crueller and more unfair treatment in print: the stories are dreams of an impossible series of revenges.

This is the sort of thing that gets criticism a bad name. Revenge is only one theme of the book among several, and the element of cruelty is in fact mild. When an enemy is defeated, the stress is not so much on his humiliation as on the ingenuity that brought it about. If the stories are to be read as something more than stories, they are best read as fictional demonstrations of cleverness defeating strength. Jack the Giant-Killer, in various forms, is a favourite Kipling type; he reappears later as Stalky himself in an Indian setting; he was very useful in an Empire of many millions under the control of some thousands. That lesson was one of the most important that Kipling learned at school.

One story, 'The Flag of his Country', might perhaps mislead the unwary reader. A pompous visiting politician harangues the boys on their duty to the Empire and is held in thorough contempt. Their feeling comes not from any lack of patriotism but from disgust at his vulgar, over-produced statement of it. The unfortunate man is in the position of a lay evangelist preaching to Jesuits.

John Kipling, finding the university in effect closed to his son, impressed by the boy's emergent literary talents, secured for him a post on an English newspaper in India. His departure was arranged for September 1882. But there had been a little more to his adolescent years than the College and visits to relatives.

Two years earlier, aged fourteen and a half, Rudyard had gone to Southsea to fetch Trix: the two sometimes spent holidays together.

Kipling matured early in physical appearance: this photograph, probably taken only a few months after the school photograph on p. 33, shows him at the time of his departure for India.

35

Edward Burne-Jones's painting of Pan and Psyche.

The confrontation with Aunty Rosa evidently passed off without the exchange of blows, but nothing is known of it. What is established is that a fifteen-year-old girl named Florence Garrard had come to board at Lorne Lodge. She had a 'Pre-Raphaelite' look – just the thing for Rudyard the youthful frequenter of the Burne-Jones circle, and he fell in love with her. Not only that: he managed to arrange several subsequent meetings, though with such Stalky-like circumspection that no details survive.

This was not just a callow yearning. The attachment was stronger on his side than hers, but it was mutual, and it persisted for some time. When he was about to return to India, he wanted them to become engaged and left under the impression that they were. Two years later she wrote to break it off; six years after that he ran into her by chance in London, found his feelings for her unchanged, took up with her again briefly, and then was rejected for good.

So nothing came of that first love, nothing except some parts of Kipling's first novel, *The Light that Failed*, written, or at any rate completed and published, in that same year, 1890. Its chief female character, Maisie, is 'founded on' Flo Garrard; how closely is unknowable, but only the most tedious kind of sceptic could doubt that Kipling was putting on paper emotions of his own when he wrote of his Dick Heldar's unhappy passion for Maisie. To say as much is not, of course, to say anything about the literary qualities of the book, and most of the events of its narrative are fictitious in the full sense, but people interested in Kipling himself, in what sort of man he was, should read it. So should people interested in novels. This one has been undervalued by critics, though, like other works of his and others' that have met the same fate, it has shown a curious knack of staying in print. Some of its weaknesses must derive from its having been written too hard upon events in its author's personal experience. I surmise that Kipling himself noticed this, or something of the sort. He never again published anything that could be referred to his sexual life.

This interlude can be extended in order to get that sexual life out of the way. To do so calls for no great earth-moving job. The known facts about Kipling's relationship with Florence Garrard are summarized above. Did he go to bed with her? Nobody knows, or is going to tell, or (I imagine) cares much either way. The same negatives apply to girls he knew in India and the United States. The known facts, similarly unsensational, of his marriage at the age of twenty-six are set out below. There are rumours, still current, that he left India littered with small brown Kiplings. This is clearly not impossible, but not nearly as probable as that there should be nebulous, unfounded rumours to that effect. Nothing contradicts the view that he was an ordinary monogamous man. If there existed real evidence to the contrary, some of it would have been sure to come out. There's no fire without smoke, and in this case there's no smoke.

To take up our story again: Rudyard, or Kipling as he had better be known from now on, landed at Bombay in October 1882 and travelled by train the thousand-odd miles to Lahore up in the north-west. Here was the museum of which his father was now Curator, a European quarter, an ancient Muslim city with liquor-shops and gambling- and opium-dens as well as palaces and mosques, a military camp, and three places of special importance to Kipling: the family bungalow, the office and print-shop of the *Civil and Military Gazette*, and the Punjab Club.

'Zam-Zammah', the great bronze gun described in the opening chapter of *Kim*, in front of the Lahore School of Art, to which Kipling's father moved in 1875 after his period in Bombay.

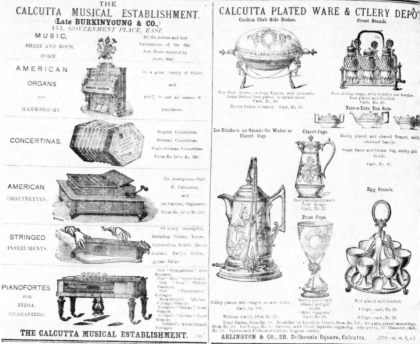

Kipling worked on the *Civil and
Military Gazette* – the paper with the
largest circulation in the Punjab –
from 1882 to 1887.

Opposite, Lahore was the capital of
the Punjab. *Above*, camel carriages
outside Government House, 1874.
Below, the Kipling family house,
a drawing by Rudyard's father.

Despite the heat, attacks of fever and dysentery, and the constant threat of typhoid, he was comfortable and happy in his parents' house. His first year was marred by periods of loneliness, with his mother off to England and his father away on leave in the hills. But at the beginning of his second, 1884, Alice returned, bringing Trix with her, and the 'Family Square' (Alice's phrase) was complete. He was secure in the constant company of three people whom he admired as well as loved, and all three of whom he came to trust as critics of his work.

Life was rather less fun at the *Gazette*, a successful daily with a large native staff and an English editor. This man, a schoolmasterly sort of person, saw to it that his new assistant did at least his fair share of the work of making up the paper and seeing it through the press. He extended this policy by often going down with fever, so that Kipling was left in sole charge. It was felt that to be kept hard at the job would be good for his character. At seventeen he was ahead of his age in some respects and very much of it in others, noisy and excitable. No doubt running or helping to run the *Gazette* was an excellent way of building up the knowledge of India that was going to make him

The Victorians took their entertainment with them to India; here Alice Kipling (*far right*) is engaged in amateur theatricals.

Opposite, Trix had been born at the Grange in June 1868.

as a writer. Other ways included night-walks in the old city after the paper had been put to bed and, starting in his second year, trips to other parts of the district to report local events: village festivals, official visits, inter-communal riots.

At the Punjab Club, the food was bad but the conversation informative to a degree that might have been designed specially for Kipling. He met those responsible for every aspect of the Imperial administration: civil servants, Army officers, doctors, lawyers, men in the departments of education, canals, forestry, engineering, irrigation, railways. They all talked shop and Kipling listened. As he noted later on a visit to Australia, you learn more from what people say to each other or take for granted than from a hundred questions.

Kipling's experience of life in this provincial centre was not confined to its upper strata. His command of the vernacular brought him into close contact with the native inhabitants of the city. And these, though predominantly Muslim, were mixed enough by religion and by race to introduce him to that limitless diversity of everything Indian which was to be one of his major themes. Another such was the common lot of the common soldier, the British ranker, whom he made it his business to get to know at Lahore. In 1885 he was admitted as a Freemason. This gave him, among who knows what else, entry into the only form of meeting-place in India where men of all castes, creeds and colours could meet as equals. If the Lahore Lodge had not existed, it would have been necessary for Kipling to invent it.

For a few weeks in the year during the hottest months, he had leave to do what everybody else did if they could and make his way up to Simla in the cool heights. This was the summer capital of the Empire, where every April the Viceroy and his staff, together with military notables, would arrive after the immense journey from Calcutta and carry on the government of the sub-continent. There was a fierce social life, with plenty of young unmarried officials and plenty of unattended married women whose husbands were sweating away at some bridge or dam on the plains: ideal conditions for intrigue, gossip, scandal, etc. For Kipling fresh from Lahore, it was 'another new world', one that never fully accepted him. It would have accepted him all right if he had stayed in India another year or two; for the time being, he was to many an inquisitive interloper with a nose for copy.

In 1886 he got back from his stay at Simla to find a new and more adventurous editor in the chair at the *Gazette*. From now on, Kipling was to abandon conventional reporting and produce weekly medium-length pieces, stories of regional life with a strong documentary interest. Verse was sometimes allowed too, as column-fillers according

Simla (*above*) lay on the slopes of the Himalayan foothills. The original hill-station was developed in a series of terraces and became an important town, in which the social pleasures were not always as formal as the picnic for the Viceroy's staff (*left*) might suggest.

43

to Kipling, but that was said so as to forestall criticism. A collection of these poems, in effect his first book, was published anonymously in a limited edition of 350 copies. It sold out quickly. A second edition, with Kipling's name on it, was issued by a Calcutta firm in the same year. *Departmental Ditties* reached London, where it failed to grip, but it was all the rage at Simla, not so much for its literary qualities as for its power to shock or titillate.

The ditties are sketches about corruption, influence, place-seeking, favouritism, flirtation and adultery in the 'bad, small world' of Anglo-India, which, as small worlds will, thought it could recognize all the characters and situations even when they were composite or fictitious. What will strike a modern reader, apart from the skill displayed, is the theme of exile and homesickness, an isolation both chafed at and jealously guarded against the interference of ignorant, incompetent outsiders – 'the travelled idiots who duly misgovern the land'.

Late the next year (1887) Kipling was promoted to the staff of a sister paper, the Allahabad *Pioneer*. It was of higher standing than the *Gazette*, with a weekly supplement which he was to edit. The move took him halfway across India to a city of largely Hindu population, despite its Muslim name. If he was lonely at first he found plenty of work to do, writing extended stories for the supplement and contributing articles based on a journey round the Native States of Rajputana in northern India. These articles, collected in his travel volumes, *From Sea to Sea*, show not only his characteristic curiosity and powers of absorption, but also a sympathetic sensitivity amazing in a man not yet twenty-three and perhaps unexpected in one so convinced of the moral justification of British power. But of that more later.

John Lockwood Kipling: a self-portrait in the form of a terracotta plaque made as a model for his own book-plate.

In January 1888 Kipling's first book of fiction, *Plain Tales from the Hills*, was published. The title perfectly suggests the straight-from-the-shoulder quality and – to a reader in England – remote setting of the contents, as well as catching the attention. (Did John Kipling suggest it? His son was for most of his life very and oddly bad at naming his works. The hand does not fly to a volume called *Actions and Reactions*. But, of course, by the time it came out – 1909 – something like *Interest Rates in Puerto Rico* would have done well enough, provided 'Rudyard Kipling' was on the title-page.)

Most of the forty *Plain Tales* had appeared first in the *Gazette*. The known fact that they were written to a length, to order, in haste, has told against them in critical esteem: they are held to be vulgar, knowing, slickly written. Anyone who was unaware of their provenance, any contemporary in England, might be forgiven for thinking the collection a work of tremendous talent, pessimistic about human behaviour,

The Pioneer.

ALLAHABAD :—MONDAY, APRIL 4, 1887. No. 7242

Vol. LXX. New Series.

CONTENTS.

[illegible]
[illegible]
The Lieutenant-Governorship of the Punjab
Public Service Commission
[illegible]
The Fatal Encounter with a Tiger
The Commander-in-Chief's Tour
Military Notes
The Duty of Cultivators in Sind
[illegible]
[illegible]
[illegible] to the East
[illegible]
A Manual [illegible] on China
The [illegible]
The Indian Medical Service
The Personnel of the Police Department
The [illegible]
Promotion in the P. W. D.
The Weather
[illegible]
Appointments, Promotions, Transfers, &c.
General Orders
Commercial
Births, Marriages, and Deaths
Shipping

LATEST TELEGRAPHIC NEWS.

REUTER'S PRESS MESSAGES.

THE IRISH CRIMES BILL.

LONDON, 2nd *April*.

In the House of Commons last night the amendment, of which Mr. Parnell had given notice, that the House should immediately go into Committee for the purpose of considering the state of Ireland, came on for discussion and led to a long and animated debate.

The Parnellites were determined to drag on the discussion, but finally Mr. W. H. Smith, First Lord of the Treasury and leader of the House, moved the *closure*, which was adopted by 361 against 253 votes.

Upon the announcement of the result of the division, Mr. Gladstone and the whole of the Radicals and Parnellites who were present left the House in a body.

The Crimes Bill was then read a first time unopposed.

GERMANY AND ALSACE.

BERLIN, 1st *April*.

M. Antoine, a Francophil member of the Reichstag for Metz, has been expelled by the German Government from Alsace.

THE ATTEMPTED ASSASSINATION OF THE CZAR.

ST PETERSBURG, 31st *March*.

The details which have been received concerning the last attempt on the Czar's life state that his Imperial Majesty was fired at by an officer in the park at Gatchina on Tuesday last, and that the bullet narrowly missed him. The would-be assassin has been arrested.

LONDON, 1st *April*.

The Bombay mails of the 18th ultimo arrived at Brindisi to-day.

THE KADIR CUP.

FROM OUR OWN CORRESPONDENT.

MEERUT, 3rd *April*.

Owing to scarcity of pig the 2nd ties only were finished on Friday and the final tie had to be run off on Saturday. 2nd heat, 2nd ties :—Captain Vesey's Sheet ; 3rd heat, Major Clowes' *Khalifa*. The final heat was won by Major Clowes on *Khalifa*.

The Pig-Hunters' Cup was afterwards run for with the following result :—Mr. Heygate's *Grumbler* 1st ; Mr. Mahon's *Amir* 2nd ; Captain Ward's *Mary Jane* 3rd.

THE RATE OF EXCHANGE IN CALCUTTA ON Saturday last was as low as 1s. $4\frac{1}{32}d$.

THE LIEUTENANT-GOVERNOR WILL LEAVE Allahabad for Lucknow on Tuesday, the 12th instant.

THE DEATH IS ANNOUNCED AT REWAH OF Sirdar Kalian Singh, one of the chief nobles of the Rewah State and the specially-appointed guardian of the young Maharaja.

LORD DUFFERIN ARRIVED AT SAHARUNPUR AT midnight on Friday. Sir Charles Aitchison on arrival from Lahore was sworn in at the railway station as a member of the Executive Council, the Viceroy, Sir Theodore Hope, Mr. Ilbert(?), and Mr. Durand, Foreign Secretary, being present.

SIR STEUART BAYLEY AND MR. J. B. LYALL assumed charge of Bengal and the Punjab respectively on Saturday. Mr. Lyall, who was staying in Allahabad, took over charge from Sir Charles Aitchison by telegraph and left in the evening for Delhi. Sir Rivers Thompson was to leave Calcutta for England yesterday afternoon. Sir Charles Aitchison leaves Delhi for Bombay, en route home, this morning.

MAHARAJA HOLKAR LEAVES BOMBAY BY THE steamer of the 29th direct for Marseilles. He proposes to stay some time in Paris and to reach England in good time for the Jubilee celebrations. Sir Lepel Griffin accompanies him on special duty with the sanction of the Viceroy, and on his suite, besides several of the officials and Sirdars, are his Secretary, Captain Norman Franks, and Dr. Caldecott, of the Central India Horse, as medical officer.

SOME FURTHER PROGRESS HAS BEEN MADE IN the latest phase of the Madras Scandals. At the Madras High Court, on Friday last, Mr. Eardley Norton resumed his application for summonses to issue in the case for damages instituted by Mr. P. Kotasawmy Tevar, the Sub-Divisional Zemindar of Ramnad, against Mr. Garstin. The Court ordered subpœnas to issue to Mr. Garstin to give evidence and produce letters ; and to the acting Chief Secretary to Government and also the Clerks of the Crown to produce certain documents and records.

WE LEARN BY TELEGRAPH FROM UMARKOT, in Lower Sind, that mass meetings of merchants and landholders were held there on the 30th and 31st ultimo and 1st instant, with a view to framing a petition to Government praying that the 240 miles of railway necessary to connect Pali, on the Rajputana State Railway, with Hyderabad in Sind, *viâ* Umarkot, be constructed. On the 2nd instant an influential deputation waited on Dr. J. Pollen, the Deputy Commissioner of Umarkot, and presented a memorial to Government stating that the proposed line offered no engineering difficulties, would prove of immense mercantile and strategic importance, and, above all, would shorten the journey between Delhi and Karachi by fifteen hours. Dr. Pollen, we are told, promised to support the memorial, adding that, as a protection against famine alone, the line should be built forthwith.

IN CONTINUATION OF OUR REMARKS IN SATURDAY'S paper on the Railway Conference held in Allahabad last week, we may state that as regards goods traffic generally the Indian Midland trains will run to the Oudh and Rohilkhand station at Cawnpore; but passengers and goods for and from stations on the East Indian line will go to the East Indian station. The Indian Midland Company, therefore, will not have a separate station at Cawnpore. The Rajputana-Malwa line may possibly have similar junction arrangements. The branch line from Mogal Sarai to the Ganges Bridge at Benares will ultimately be transferred by the East Indian Railway to Government and by the latter to the Oudh and Rohilkhand Company, but the E. I. R. will of course retain and work the Mogal Sarai junction on the main line.

THE SOUTHERN SHANS SEEM TO BE GIVING trouble in Burma. At Sinthawa on the Sittang River, near Nyingyan, a band is reported to have attacked the post, but to have been easily repulsed. Further south, however, in the Tenasserim Division the raiders have been more successful, 200 houses in the flourishing town of Hlineboay having been burnt. As in previous cases in Lower Burma the majority of the Burman police behaved in a cowardly manner. A detachment of 25 Punjabi police has been hurriedly sent from Moulmein to Hlineboay, but they will scarcely suffice to pursue the Shans, if the latter are in any numbers. There is not much news from Upper Burma. The Wuntho Tsawbwa, having made full and complete submission, is to be left to govern his State as a tributary Chief, our troops retiring to Kawlin, twelve miles to the south.

A STARTLING MURDER, WHICH IS ATTRIBUTED to the robber-leader Tantia, and which, if correctly so attributed, testifies to his extreme audacity, is reported from Khargaon. The operations for the capture of this notorious freebooter have been placed by Government in the hands of the Agent to the Governor-General in Central India, and detachments from the Central India Horse, the Malwa-Bhil Corps, and the Bhopal Battalion are now engaged in attempting to capture Tantia. On the morning of the 24th ultimo a Mahratta sepoy, named Ganpat, belonging to the expedition, was found missing on the roll of the Malwa-Bhil Corps being called. Search was made and the body of the missing sepoy was found on the bank of the Dipa River. He had been murdered by strangulation: his hands were tied behind his back, and in addition to marks of strangling there were three wounds on his body—one on the neck, one on the skull, and the third on the face. His purse was empty, and he had apparently been robbed as well as murdered. Only conjecture attaches this murder to Tantia. It seems rather to resemble a case of thagi, which may possibly survive in these remote districts.

THE FOLLOWING PARAGRAPH APPEARS IN ONE of the papers by the last Mail: "A woman, named Corrigan, residing near Doura, County Leitrim, has been delivered of four children at a birth—three girls and a boy. They are all doing well. The family are miserably poor, the father being a small farmer. The children lie on straw, covered with rags, beside the fire. The landlord has forgiven the father a year's rent in consideration of the increase of the family." The landlord's heart is good, but his political economy is bad. No doubt it is well in certain cases that it should be so: the Arab proverb tells us that the eye of the heart can see further than the eye of the head; but men should not be encouraged to multiply instances where the head is put into antagonism with the heart, and the multiplication of babies by a starving man is the multiplication of such instances. Instead of remitting one year's rent to the wretched Leitrim farmer, Mr. Cotter Morison would put him in prison. We would not do this, firstly, because the Leitrim farmer is an ignorant man who has never heard of political economy and can scarcely be blamed for not understanding the principles on which a standard of comfort can be attained; and, secondly, because we should be punishing the wrong man. The true criminals are those who have been telling the Leitrim farmer for years that all his miseries come from the landlord and the English Government, and that were it not for them a life of comfort would be assured. What on earth can a dozen Land Bills do in a case like cottier Corrigan's? The remission of a year's rent? The gift of the holding and the throwing-in of the one adjoining would hardly touch the evil.

IN NO PART OF UPPER BURMA IS THE SUCCESS we have obtained more marked than in Bhamo. The whole of the arrangements there reflect the greatest credit on Mr. Burgess and Major Adamson, the Civil Officers. After the attack on the stockade and the murder of a British non-commissioned officer in the Chinese quarter last December strong measures were taken. The quarter was searched for arms, and one Chinese headman was fined Rs. 3,000 for having guns and ammunition hidden in his house. The Chinese on this closed their shops; two days afterwards a pork-vendor complained that his stock had been seized by the orders of the Chinese. The ringleader this time was brought up for theft and punished as a common thief, and the Bhamo Chinese difficulty was over. The next day the Chinese reopened their shops and have been doing a flourishing trade since. The Shans in the town are daily increasing in numbers, some 200 families having had quarters allotted to them in the past few months. The trade with China is rapidly increasing, and the Ka-Chins who were formerly hostile to the Burmese are friendly to us and largely employed on public works. Danger is always to be feared by the assembling of outlaws and blackguards from both China and Burma in the Ka-Chin hills, where they are at all times on the look-out for opportunities to burn and plunder. But as the Ka-Chins get more civilised and friendly to us this danger will be minimised, and they will cease to be the victims of any plausible scoundrel pretending to be working for either the Chinese Government or some Burman prince. The appointment to Bhamo of Mr. Baber and Mr. Warry, officers well acquainted with the Chinese and their ways, is also a guarantee that the frontier policy will be a sound and consistent one.

Apropos OF TO-DAY'S TELEGRAM ANNOUNCING the expulsion from Alsace of one of the Separatist members of the Reichstag returned at the late elections, it is interesting to note the present attitude of the French Republic on the question of the Rhine Provinces as we find it described by the Editor of the *République Française* in the current number of the *Nineteenth Century*. M. Joseph Reinach is filled with grief and amazement at the idea of Englishmen believing that a "well-bred and well-mannered" nation like *La Grande République* could think of disturbing the peace of Europe, and he takes pains to show that the recent war scare was all Bismarck's doing. The article is not very convincing. Possibly M. Reinach is right in saying that France has had no thought of war within the last year: a man may take off his coat and tuck up his shirt-sleeves, and yet be disagreeably surprised if someone interprets this to mean fight and acts accordingly; but the man with the coat off risks a row, and France most distinctly had her coat off and was talking *à la* Bob Acres before the duel, until one morning the Berlin correspondents of the Paris papers telegraphed that Bismarck had been speaking of "*saigner la France à blanc*," on which sparring with the air ceased and there was a great silence. At any rate whatever France meant at the opening of the year, M. Reinach certainly says nothing to show she will not go to war when a favourable opportunity occurs. For one thing he does not even attempt to explain the enthusiasm of the Republic for melenite, mammoth mortars, and colossal army votes; but his embarrassment is most apparent when he comes to deal specifically with the Reichsland question. M. Reinach says every Frenchman respects the Treaty of Frankfort, and declares in the same breath that no Frenchman will yield his country's right to Alsace-Lorraine. Between these two he thinks there is all the difference that separates legality from disgrace. This is certainly subtle. By the Treaty France yields the Provinces for ever: according to M. Reinach, Frenchmen respect the Treaty: and yet no Frenchman will admit that he bows to its provisions. M. Reinach in fact really implies that in the view of all Frenchmen there is no difference at all between legality and disgrace in the case of the Frankfort Treaty. In the Place de la Concorde at Paris one may see an allegorical figure of Strasbourg covered with wreaths and with the subscription, "*Qui vive? La France*"—a truly pathetic sight. M. Reinach thinks one might as justly ask France to suppress this statue as to say she renounces Alsace-Lorraine. The cases, however, are hardly parallel. In the one France is merely asked to give an assurance that she stands by the Treaty supposed to define her relations with Germany; in the other she would be offered a needless and uncalled-for affront. Bismarck is not careful of sentiment when it stands in his way; but he does not trample on it without reason, and he is not given to petty insults. We do not say that France is altogether blameworthy in refusing to regard the Frankfort Treaty as final; what we do say is that her refusal is a constant source of danger to the peace of Europe, which any occasion may convert into the cause of actual rupture. Contrary to his intention, M. Reinach has become a witness on the same side.

that morning seemed to take hours, and when at
last I had got myself dressed somehow, I dared
not look in the glass because I knew a scare-crow
would be nothing to my appearance.

I cannot attempt to describe that walk ; in fact,
all the recollection I have of it is that in my
hurry I had put my boots on to the wrong feet
and returned quite lame in consequence. I did
not properly wake up until we had turned to go
home again, and when at last I re-entered the
house it was with such a headache as I had never
had before and hope never to have again. I
stayed in bed all that day, and had not even the
spirit to answer John when he said, the last thing
at night, with a malicious smile: " I suppose you
are going to get up early again to-morrow ?"

　　　　　　　　　　　　　　　　　　　P.

THE SONG OF THE WOMEN.

" Our feelings in this matter are shared by thousands
and thousands of our sisters throughout the land—and of
this we are assured by many signs not likely to come under
the observation of the outside world."—*Vide Address of the
Women of Utterpara to Lady Dufferin.*

How shall she know the worship we would do her?
　The walls are high and she is very far.
How can the women's message reach unto her
　Above the tumult of the packed bazar?
　　Free Wind of Chait, against the lattice blow-
　　　ing,
　　Bear thou our thanks lest she depart unknow-
　　　ing.

Go forth across the fields we may not roam in—
　Go forth beyond the trees that rim the city—
To whatsoe'er fair place she hath her home in
　Who dowered us with wealth of help and pity.
　　Out of our shadow pass and seek her singing:—
　　" I bear no gifts but Love alone for bringing."

Say that we be a feeble folk who greet her,
　But old in grief and very wise in tears,
Say that we, being desolate, entreat her
　That she forget us not in after years;
　　For we have looked on light and it were grievous
　　To dim that dawning if our Lady leave us.

The consort of a ruler—more than human—
　Remote, unseen, a gracious mane alone?
Nay surely, for we know her very woman
　Who, stooping down, hath made our woe her own.
　　Fear not, O Wind, but swiftly follow after,
　　And take our cry, half weeping and half
　　　laughter.

By Life that passed with none to stay the failing,
　By Love's sad springs garnered ere the spring,
When Love-in-Ignorance wept unavailing
　O'er young buds dead before the blossoming.
　　By all the *purdah* cloaked, the cold moon
　　　viewed
　　In past grim years, declare our gratitude.

By hands uplifted to the Gods that heard not,
　By gifts that found no favour in their sight,
By faces bent above the babe that stirred not,
　By nameless horrors of the stifling night,
　　By ills foredone—by peace her toils discover—
　　Bid Earth be good beneath and Heaven above
　　　her.

If she have sent her servants in our pain,
　If she have fought with Death and dulled his
　　sword,
If she have given back our sick again,
　And to our breast the weakling lips restored,
　　Is it a little thing that she hath wrought?
　　Then Birth and Death and Motherhood be
　　　naught.

Go forth, O Wind, the message on thy wings,
　And they shall hear thee pass and bid thee speed,
In reed-roofed hut or white-walled home of kings,
　Who have been holpen by her in their need.
　　All Spring shall give thee fragrance, and the
　　　wheat
　　Shall be a golden floorcloth to thy feet.

Haste, for our hearts are with thee—take no rest.
　Clear voiced ambassador from sea to sea,
Proclaim the blessing manifold, confessed,
　Of those in darkness by her hand set free.
　　Then very softly to her Presence move,
　　And whisper :—" Lady! Lo, they know and
　　　love !"

　　　　　　　　　　　　　　　　　　　R. K.

KAISER WILHELM.

Hark, the tramp of armed battalions,
　Marching on with measured tread !
See the silent thousands standing,
　Bidding farewell to the dead !

Agéd warrior, King and Kaiser
　Now at last Life's victory's won,
And a grateful people bless thee
　For thy work so nobly done.

Fit successor of the hero,
　Known a thousand years to fame,
Thou hast been the second founder
　Of our country's perished name !

Germans, *once again* a nation,
　Bid your Kaiser now farewell ;
Germans and the world for ever
　Kaiser Wilhelm's tale will tell !

Father of our German nation,
　Now around thy bier we stand ;
Father, be thy spirit present
　E'er to guard our Fatherland !

　　　　　　　　　　　　　　　　　　　C. D.

THE SEASON.

THE weekly summary of the provincial reports
on the weather and prospects of the crops is as
follows :—

MADRAS.—For week ending 7th April.—No rain
except a small quantity in Ganjam, Vizagapatam,
Bellary, Tinnevelly, and Malabar. Rainfall to date
generally sufficient, except in parts of Vizagapatam,
North Arcot, Tirchinopoly, Madura, Tinnevelly,
Coimbatore, Nilgiris, and Salem. Crops generally
good, but very slightly damaged by insects in
Trichinopoly, and withering in parts of Madura,
Tinnevelly, and Coimbatore. Pasture generally
sufficient, but scanty in Malabar, Nilgiris, and parts
of Madura and Anantapur, and decreasing in Vizagapatam, North Arcot, Trichinopoly, Coimbatore, and
Salem. Prices rising where not stationary. General
prospects favourable.

BOMBAY.—For week ending 11th April.—Slight
rain in parts of Dharwar and Sholapur. Standing
crops in good condition. Cotton-picking continues
in parts of Guzerat and Southern Mahratta Country.
Harvesting of late crops completed in Kolaba and
Baroda, and in progress in other districts. Ploughing
operations for next season's crops in progress in
Kurrachee, Hyderabad, Broach, Nasik, Thana, Ratna-
giri, Poona, Ahmednagar, Sholapur, Satara, Bijapur,
Belgaum, Kanara, and Wadhwan. Probable outturn
of late crops from 10 to 14 annas in Poona and from
6 to 10 annas in Baroda.

BENGAL.—For week ending 10th April.—A few
light showers are reported in South-West and East
Bengal and in the Balasore and Singhboom districts.
Rain is wanted throughout the Bhagalpur division,
and in parts of the Orissa, Burdwan, Presidency, and
Rajshahye divisions. Ploughing and sowing of autumn crops are proceeding on. Prospects of spring
rice continue favourable. Indigo seedlings are doing
well. Sugarcane is being planted. *Mahua* is expected to be a good crop, except in Bhagalpur. Rabi
harvest is nearly over. The outturn is generally
good, but is below the average in parts of the Bhagalpur and Chota Nagpur divisions. No marked fluc-
tuation in the price of common rice during the past
fortnight.

NORTH-WESTERN PROVINCES AND OUDH.—For
week ending 11th April.—Weather seasonable. Crops
nearly all harvested, outturn good. Sugarcane is
being sown and irrigated. Indigo sowing has com-
menced. Opium collection is nearly finished. Mar-
kets are well stocked, and prices are steady. The
condition of stock cattle is generally good.

PUNJAB.—For week ending 11th April.—Slight rain
in Ferozepore. Prices are somewhat unsettled ; in
two districts, a rise is reported, and in others prices
falling or stationary. Kharif ploughings and sugarcane and cotton sowings in progress. Harvesting
of rabi crops and collection of gram and barely com-
menced. Rabi prospects are reported good, except
in Shahpur, where they are below average, and in
Rawalpindi and Peshawar, where they are average.
Slight damage done to rabi crops in Sirsa tahsil on
account of hail, and also in Jullundur for want of
rain. Stock of cattle are generally healthy. Poppy
crop average.

CENTRAL PROVINCES.—For week ending 11th
April.—Weather hot. Threshing of winter crops
continues, outturn good. Fields are being manured
in Bilaspur for rain weather sowings. Sugarcane
thriving. Cattle in fair condition.

BURMA.—For week ending 7th April.—Prospects
of dry weather crops continue to be satisfactory.
Condition of agricultural stock generally good.

A Kipling contribution to *The
Pioneer Mail*, 'The Song of the
Women', April 1888.

'Your potery very good, Sir; just coming proper length to-day': the standards of Indian journalism were not always literary; illustration from Jerome K. Jerome's *My First Book*.

certainly, often designed to appeal to the reader's more malicious instincts, well yes, but wise as well as worldly-wise, full of atmosphere, touching, harrowing, comic, and inflexibly just to the 'natives', who are portrayed on the whole as worthier than the Anglo-Indians they encounter. Kipling was to write better stories than any of these, but no subsequent volume so consistent in quality.

To be sure, these are anecdotes: how a subaltern's suicide was covered up, how a horse-race was fixed, how a woman won her husband back from a rival, how a bank manager prevented his unpleasant assistant from dying in misery, how a colour-sergeant's wife set an example in a cholera outbreak, how a Hindu girl was punished for having an affair with an Englishman. But the last-

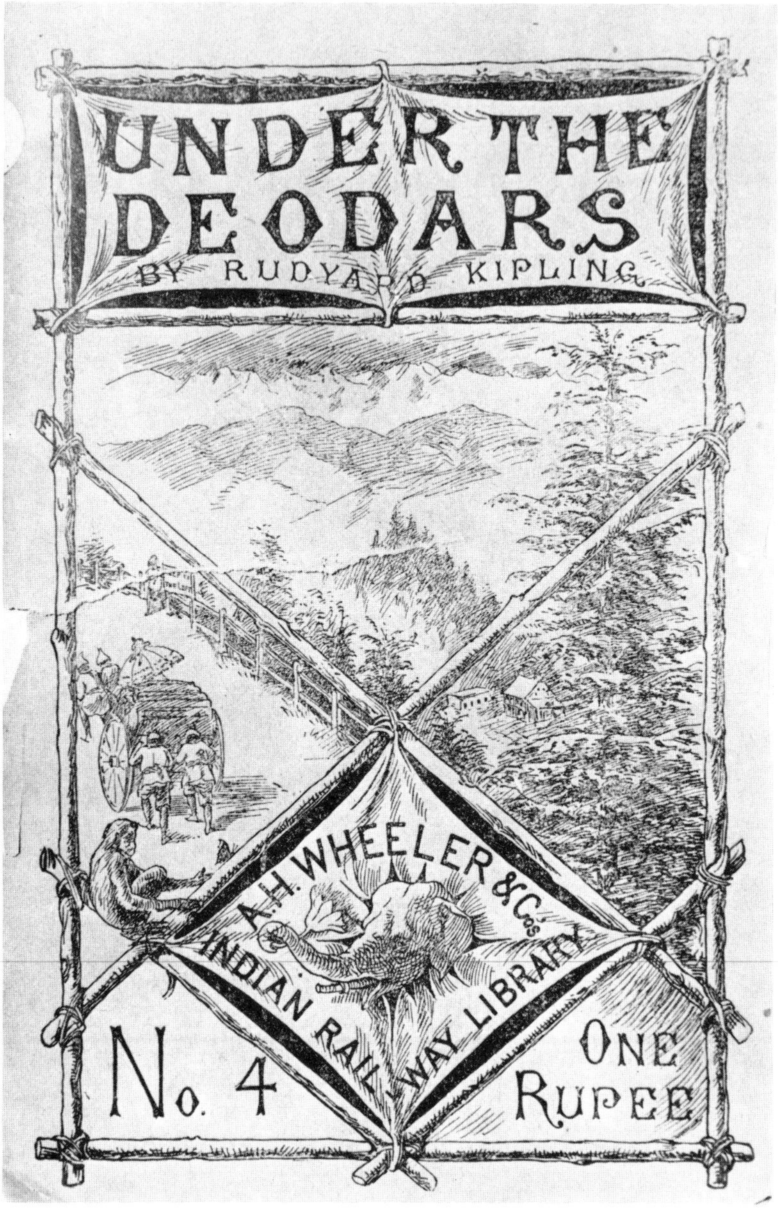

Right and opposite, Indian Railway Library editions first popularized Kipling.

alluded-to, 'Beyond the Pale', is one of the most terrible stories in the language, and even the slighter themes contribute to the whole: the book *is* a whole, a composite portrait of Anglo-Indian life such as its author could not possibly have foreseen when he was scribbling off each item in the newspaper office. Not very likely, at least.

The *Plain Tales* soon sold out in India, but hung fire in London. Kipling's new stories for the *Pioneer* were being collected in successive

PRICE ONE SHILLING

THE PHANTOM RICKSHAW
& other EERIE TALES
by Rudyard Kipling

A H Wheeler & Co's
Indian
Railway Library
No 5 One Rupee No 5

LAHORE

LONDON:
SAMPSON LOW, MARSTON & COMPANY,
Limited,
St. Dunstan's House, Fetter Lane, Fleet Street E.C

paperbacks and marketed by the Indian Railway Library. So his fame spread through India and beyond, because railway travellers take books home, even when 'home' is as far as England. He was writing away, off on a trip for the *Pioneer* that took him down to Calcutta, where he was impressed chiefly by the heat, the night, the stink, and the efficiency of the police. The city was the administrative centre of British India, the abode of remote officialdom where no real work was done.

Simla: the Town Hall and Mall in
the 1890s.

Kipling's travels in India were helped
greatly by the railways, in spite of
difficulties created by the terrain; here,
the 'Agony Point' on the Darjeeling
Railway.

He returned to Allahabad, was called back to Lahore to relieve the editor of the *Gazette*, and went up to Simla on his last visit. Now he was determined to leave for England, for London where there was 'some place to go every night' if one cared to – and where there was also the centre of the English-speaking literary world. At Simla there came what he called the proudest moment of his life, when the Commander-in-Chief India consulted him about the *real* state of feeling among the rank and file. He was still only twenty-two years old. But, as in his adolescence, he looked substantially older than his age, an attribute worth bearing in mind – remotely, perhaps – when considering Kipling's experiences as a young man.

Characteristically, and luckily for us, he decided not to go home the conventional way, through the Suez Canal, but via the Far East, the United States and the Atlantic. The success of the railway publications had brought him enough money to get to England; in the company of an American couple, he sailed from Calcutta in March 1889. He was to make one brief return visit, but in effect this was for him the last of India.

India and Kipling had been made for each other. She gave him what no other English writer was ever to experience in comparable fullness

Old Court House Street, Calcutta, in the 1880s.

The impact of India: statue of a deity from Kipling's country home, Bateman's.

India on the brain; cartoon of
Kipling, c. May 1892.

RUDYARD KIPLING

INDIAN TALES

Abridged and supplied with
Vocabulary by
M. LORIE

K

STATE TEXT-BOOK PUBLISHING HOUSE OF
THE PEOPLE'S COMMISSARIAT OF EDUCATION OF THE R. S. F. S. R.
MOSCOW — 1940

Kipling's popularity has not been
confined to the Western 'imperialist'
countries: title-page of Russian
translation of *Indian Tales*, 1940.

and intensity; he brought to her exactly those gifts which were
necessary to commemorate, in the words of an Indian writer, Nirad C.
Chaudhuri, 'the many faces of [that] country in all their beauty,
power and truth'. And her mark was set on him for life: with the
exception of some travel pieces, seven or eight stories and a few dozen
poems (not a large exception in the case of such a copious author) all
his best work reflects or remembers India.

His years there had also formed his outlook on the world, his beliefs,
his politics. All this may seem a large subject; it certainly seemed so
to critics in his lifetime and in the period immediately following.
As one of them wrote, 'It would be quite impossible not to make
politics a great part of any book about Kipling.' No doubt it was then,
in 1940. But, with the passing of the Empire, that impossibility has
passed too. Chaudhuri could see in 1957 that Kipling's politics
were 'no essential ingredient of his writings', or, more sharply, that
'It is the easiest thing to wash out the free acid of Kiplingian politics
from his finished goods.'* With some of the better-known verse, at
least, it may not be quite so easy, and some précis of the beliefs of a
writer so interested in beliefs seems called for.

Kipling was an authoritarian in the sense that he was not a democrat.
To him, a parliament was a place where people with no knowledge
of things as they were could dictate to the men who did real work, and
could change their dictates at whim. His ideal was a feudalism that
had never existed, a loyal governed class freely obeying incorrupt,
conscientious governors. He was vague about how you became a
governor: you probably (as in the Empire) just found you were one.
Nevertheless, birth, influence, money, educational status and the like
must not count as qualifications for leadership. Merit, competence
and a sense of responsibility were what did count: 'the job belongs to
the man who can do it'. As George Orwell pointed out, Kipling was
further from being a fascist than can easily be imagined in a period
when totalitarianism – a very different thing from authoritarianism – is
accepted as a possibly valid or even desirable system. He (Kipling) was
that nowadays puzzling creature, an oligarch who believed passion-
ately in freedom.

Kipling was an imperialist. He accepted the Empire as it stood and
he approved the annexation of Upper Burma. His position has been
explained semi-mystically (the Empire was justified because it
fostered virtue in its administrators) and psychologically (the Empire

* Kipling's politics have evidently not bothered his millions of foreign readers. The Russians,
for instance, while keen on their own imperialism whether of Tsarist or Soviet stamp, have
never cared for that of other nations. Nevertheless, Kipling's popularity with them is legendary.
The poet Yevgeny Yevtushenko roared with laughter when I suggested that Kipling might be
too 'imperialist' for his taste, and immediately recited to me a large part of 'Boots' in Russian
translation. I forgot to ask him what he thought of *Kim*.

was attractive because it was an island of security in a turbulent, hostile universe). Either or both may be well founded, though our understanding of the matter is not much deepened. Kipling had seen the Empire in action; he knew the disinterested devotion whereby much of its work was done; he knew too the dire forces – banditry, massacre, flood, drought, famine, plague – which would be loosed if its authority were to fail. (He was generally an accurate prophet.) The Empire was riddled with imperfections, and it neither would nor should last for ever. But there were limits to his objectivity; some of his admirations were uncritical. This would not matter in the least if he had kept it out of his work. Unfortunately he could not altogether. There is one type, usually a subaltern, who keeps coming up in the stories: brave, modest and artless. The bravery is all right, but the other two qualities are sometimes pushed to the brink of farce or horror. This figure appears notably in 'A Conference of the Powers', where he piles on the agony by constantly forgetting not to use vernacular terms to an uncomprehending London novelist. The story is always cited by those who feel that Kipling betrayed his art to his political ideas.

Kipling was a racialist, or racist. The White Man's Burden is indeed a burden, an arduous duty, not the inheritance of a natural

Proclamation of Queen Victoria as Empress of India, Delhi, January 1877. Kipling's father was entrusted by the Viceroy with the design of the emblazoned banners of the Indian princes at the durbar or public audience.

privilege, and the white men must carry it not because they are white but because they are qualified; for instance, the Americans in the Philippines must govern their 'new-caught, sullen peoples, half devil and half child' who cannot govern themselves. This is a limited racialism: white men, in practice those whose native tongue is English, are good at exercising authority in beneficent ways and have the wherewithal – medicine, transport systems, law-enforcement – to do it. Other races may well be good at other things, and their rights and customs must in any event and at all times be scrupulously respected. Among them are many individuals who are superior to many white men, and a white degenerate is always worse than any other kind. All the same, Kipling believed in the separation, or rather the continued separateness, of races. *—

– Racial separateness, for Kipling, was not to exclude cordial and mutually respectful dealings in the way of work or on certain social occasions. It must be voluntary, a matter of shared custom, not enforced: nobody would have been a more convinced or educated opponent of *apartheid* than he. But as regards sexual dealings: 'A man should, whatever happens, keep to his own caste, race, and breed.— Let the White go to the White and the Black to the Black' – unless he wants a disaster. This is an appeal to prudence rather than prejudice, as he goes on to demonstrate (in 'Beyond the Pale').

Most of the ignorant castigation of Kipling as a racialist in the full aggressive sense comes from a single famous line of verse quoted out of context:

Oh, East is East and West is West and never the twain shall meet,

which is followed by the qualification:

Till Earth and Sky stand presently at God's great Judgment Seat;

which in turn leads to the antithesis:

But there is neither East nor West, Border, nor Breed, nor Birth,
When two strong men stand face to face, though they come from the
   ends of the Earth!

This, however, is not a complete antithesis. What about more than two men, or not-so-strong men, or men just standing about instead of face to face? The twain shall meet only under exceptional conditions. Yet meet they shall. Ifs and buts are bound to clog any treatment of this matter. All that is clear is that Kipling understood and honoured men of other races more deeply than any other English writer, as a reading of *Kim* will suggest.

'A young man . . . walking slowly at the head of his flocks, while at his knee ran small naked Cupids.' Illustration of 'William the Conqueror' from *The Day's Work*, in *The Kipling Reader* (1908).

* Throughout this section, as elsewhere, my attempt is to explain what he believed, not to condemn or, on other points, to defend those beliefs, and certainly not to put him right on facts.

The Law of the European in action: 'Our Judge', illustration from *Curry and Rice* by G. F. Atkinson (1911).

Kipling was a paternalist. This is an ugly word with, nowadays, an ugly connotation it does not deserve. Any father who loves his children, as he did, will expect them to accede to his authority while they remain children, but he will discharge his responsibilities to them, keep order between them, train them, try to teach them all he knows and recognize, it may be unwillingly, that the day will come when they must stand on their own feet. He had better not look for thanks.

Kipling believed in something ill-defined, though practical and unmysterious, called 'The Law'. It pervades his *Jungle Books*, but it has nothing to do with the law of the jungle as we usually think of it (that is, the weak finish last). What is envisaged is society as a network of obligations, each individual doing the job appropriate to him to the best of his ability. Law, order, duty, restraint, obedience, discipline (to tidy up a line from a poem) may sound to us in combination like the programme of some right-wing political adventurer; for Kipling they were values to be pursued freely, at the bidding of self-respect and self-reliance. Their message is, of course, a conservative one, without much application to our time.

Kipling spent his journey to England in mixed states of feeling. Shipboard life was fun and there was the ship itself to be explored thoroughly, most of all below decks, where the real work went on. Some of the places visited on the way disturbed him. Burma had attractive women, but too many sinister Chinamen, and the whole place seemed too Oriental. 'Singapur' struck him as very unhealthy; 'I want to go Home! I want to go back to India! I am miserable', he cried, or rather wrote in one of the travel articles he sent back to the

Pioneer. Hong Kong brought more Chinese, all working like fury.
At this stage China itself ought to be annexed, he considered, but a
short trip to Canton suggested to him a better course would be to
'kill off' the whole nation. They had frightened him, a rare achievement, not by overt menace but by the universal contempt they exuded.

Japan, where Kipling spent a month, was a different matter, neat
and beautiful, with gentle, gracious people who yet had 'a strain of
bloodthirstiness' in them. The main trouble with them was that,
under American influence, they had adopted a constitution and a
parliament. He predicted serious mischief when all that had had time
to work. Despite these forebodings, he was enchanted by the country,
and some of his most vivid travel writing comes from his stay there.

So at last to San Francisco, 'a mad city' with shootings in the
streets and rude hotel clerks. Everybody talked with an American
accent, started getting drunk at 10.30 a.m. and had the vote. The
women were free and lively, the men tough, masculine and generous,
the children very spoilt. After a visit to Vancouver, where it was
quieter and more civilized, Kipling returned to the United States.
At Omaha he found detestable burial customs, embalmed bodies in
backless dress-suits looking out through the windows of their coffins
half a century before Evelyn Waugh came along. Americans were
friendly and honest, also ignorant, 'cocksure, lawless and casual'.
They were always running down their own country in conversation
and praising it embarrassingly. 'I love this people,' Kipling summed
up.

57

It must be remembered that he was not only new to America but also, until he reached the Pacific on his journey there, to Americans in any number. His reactions show an honest confusion of mind, and an eye for contradictions, rather than any instability of mood or see-saw of experience. He was never able to make out quite what he felt about the country and its inhabitants; his admiration and disgust were equally genuine. This conflict was to become important when he settled in the US three years later. Very early on this first visit, he noted an anti-British sentiment which he interpreted as a cohesive force among a nation still struggling to absorb a great wave of immigrants from many parts of Europe.

In October 1889, when he was not quite twenty-four years old, Kipling arrived in London. He was not unknown from the outset, his cousins visited him, he made new literary contacts, joined the Savile Club, began to be published in England and to move on his rapid march to fame. But he was lonely, ailing and depressed, missing India and the sun, suspicious of the prevailing current of artistic talk and behaviour. With all his knowledge of the outside world, he was a colonial in the London of the English Decadence, on the eve of the Nineties and *The Picture of Dorian Gray*. The gulf never narrowed: indeed it widened. Kipling was sneered at as an upstart and a philistine, most effectively by Max Beerbohm; and he returned the sneers.

Immigrants in Battery Park, New York, April 1896. Kipling reacted strongly against the lawlessness and squalor – and the extravagance – of New York. 'The more one studied it, the more grotesquely bad it grew.'

There was soon to be trouble over copyrights in the United States, especially bothersome to an unbusinesslike young man short of money.

Some of this put itself right over the following few months, though the unsuccessful encounter with Flo Garrard in the spring could hardly have cheered him up. He was writing and being printed at top speed; by the end of 1890 he was famous in England and America. His Barrack-Room Ballads and a number of stories had come out in periodicals, *The Times* had pronounced favourably and at length on *Plain Tales from the Hills*, he had finished and published (in the US) *The Light that Failed*, and his Indian Railway Library tales had appeared in collected editions as *Soldiers Three* and *Wee Willie Winkie*.

Overleaf, Indian Railway Library covers for *Soldiers Three* and *Wee Willie Winkie*.

PRICE ONE SHILLING.

SOLDIERS THREE

No. 1 BY

Rudyard Kipling

ONE RUPEE.

A.H. WHEELER & Cos
INDIAN RAILWAY LIBRARY

LAHORE

LONDON:
SAMPSON LOW, MARSTON, SEARLE, & RIVINGTON, Ld.,
ST. DUNSTAN'S HOUSE, FETTER LANE, E.C.
NEW YORK: BROMFIELD & CO., 658 BROADWAY.

WEE WILLIE WINKIE
and other Stories
by Rudyard Kibling.

A. H. Wheeler & Co.s
Indian Railway Library
No. 6 (One Rupee

LONDON:
SAMPSON LOW, MARSTON & COMPANY,
Limited,
St. Dunstan's House, Fetter Lane, Fleet Street, E.C.

The last two volumes contain little of Kipling's best work. The soldiers – Mulvaney the Irishman, Learoyd the Yorkshireman and Ortheris the Cockney – had not yet come to their maturity; here, for the most part, Mulvaney recounts long, not very funny anecdotes in Irish dialect, every other word conscientiously mutilated by an apostrophe or a would-be phonetic spelling. The result is occasionally inaccurate and inconsistent and always, now that custom has swung away from close representation of speech-sounds, rather difficult to read. The volume also contains an unsuccessful experiment in play-script form and a number of stories that have earned their subsequent neglect.

Wee Willie Winkie (honestly, what a title!) consists first of pieces that might be called fancy tales from the hills about amours and adulteries at Simla and elsewhere. They lack the economy and force of the earlier stories, and are written in a cheaply urbane style that, together with the setting and subject-matter, might make the unversed reader mistake them for the work of Somerset Maugham on an off-day. Kipling saw – or his mother told him – that this sort of thing was not his forte and he never again attempted it.

Four of the stories, including the eponymous one, are about young children. Two of them are little monsters of whimsy, their infantile dialect reproduced with a fidelity, or at least an assiduity, that raises the hair:

'Yeth! And Chimo [the spaniel] to sleep at ve foot of ve bed, and ve pink pikky-book, and ve bwead – 'cause I will be hungwy in ve night – and vat's all, Miss Biddums . . .'

Black Sheep turns up here too, and childish honour is only rescued by the two young heroes of the rousing battle-piece that closes the volume.

Also included is the grossly overrated long tale, 'The Man Who Would Be King'. The man, or as it turns out the men (there are two of them), would attain royal status among some tribe beyond the hills, it seems by the merest cunning and effrontery. This silly prank ends in predictable and thoroughly deserved disaster. One of the aspirants is killed by the indignant natives, the other crawls back to Lahore or somewhere and survives just long enough to tell the tale to a news-paperman whom it is convenient to call Kipling.

The telling of the story is very full and detailed, despite its teller's reduced condition and the tiresome wanderings of mind so caused. Earlier, before setting off on their antic, he and his comrade have been no more than intolerably garrulous in telling Kipling the first part of their tale, what they mean to do and something of why, and there is an earlier part still in which one of these buffoons long-windedly asks Kipling to take a message to the other. Much is made intermediately of the newspaper-office setting.

Terracotta plaque made by John Lockwood Kipling to illustrate 'The Man Who Would Be King'.

    This is a story with an unusually elaborate frame even for Kipling, who was much too fond of the device. The elaboration has fooled critics, who mistake it for complexity, which they are used to mistaking for profundity. In this case they are given considerable help by the notion of kingship, one with just the right degree of cloudy importance to encourage talk of what it might or might not stand for, be or not be a metaphor of, etc. The discipline of writing to a length and a time-limit, as with the *Plain Tales*, may be good training; its removal may lead to self-indulgence.

Nothing so sternly pedagogical need be said of the stories written in London and collected in *Life's Handicap*. 'The Courting of Dinah Shadd' and 'On Greenhow Hill' reintroduce the Soldiers and make suffering human beings of two of them; the frame-device also reappears, but trimmed down in both and properly related to the main narrative in the latter. 'Without Benefit of Clergy' starts off as an account of a liaison between an Englishman and a native girl but, unlike 'Beyond the Pale', a harsher treatment of a similar theme, turns into an unsentimental elegy for all doomed love. We might be tempted to see in the two horror stories, 'The Mark of the Beast' and 'At the End of the Passage', a reflection of the author's own low spirits at the time of writing, if we did not know how often low spirits in the self produce high spirits on paper.

The Barrack-Room Ballads were a quite new venture, indeed without precedent (or descendant) in English poetry as regards both style and content. The Cockney dialect and the heavy rhythms of the music-hall song were used for serious purposes, and the life of the common soldier furnished the themes: parades, women, action, beer, leave, natives, officers, NCOs, sun, cholera, cells, discharge. Out of these conventionally unpromising elements Kipling produced among others the most harrowing poem in our language ('Danny Deever') and a love lyric ('Mandalay') unique for what a critic in 1900 called its 'wonderful transmuting use of the commonest material'. A powerful underlying message of the Ballads is that freedom, order, art, learning and everything we call civilization depends in the last resort on the activities of a few score thousand commonplace, ignorant, vulgar, violent men whom it is all too easy to despise. Tommy Atkins's sardonic comment on the cheapness of 'making mock of uniforms that guard you while you sleep' has a formidable relevance today. It was good then too.

The success of the Ballads was immediate; after their first book-publication a couple of years later, it started to become widespread to a degree surpassed only by that of Shakespeare (and Anon.). Before the end of the century the poems were being recited or sung in music-halls and at smoking-concerts. If, as has been suggested, they put forward an officer-class view of the private soldier, the ranker class in civilian clothes did not much care or notice.

Soon after arriving in London, Kipling had met a young American publisher called Wolcott Balestier. He had literary ambitions,

among which was writing a novel in collaboration with Kipling, an unlikely project, it might be thought, given the latter's determined self-sufficiency. But he took to Balestier, as most people did, and for the next year and a half enjoyed with him the closest friendship of his life. The novel, *The Naulahka*, was written and eventually published. (The title refers to a fabulous necklace.) It is by no means a bad book. The first four chapters, certainly Balestier's work, show an engaging light wit that Kipling never attempted. If the former used the same sort of style in talk as in writing, we have a good unsensational reason for the latter's attachment to him.

More to the point: in the autumn of 1890 Kipling met a girl three years older than himself, Caroline Balestier, Wolcott's sister, who was over in England with her mother and the other sister. 'Carrie' was to become Kipling's wife. She was small (the right size for him), energetic, competent and protective; she came from a 'good' Vermont family and, as the sister of a valued friend, might have seemed very suitable. Evidently Kipling's parents, in London on a visit, did not think so. The tradition is that, at first sight of Carrie, Alice said,

Opposite, Carrie Kipling. The marriage ceremony with Rudyard was a bizarre one, the celebrations affected by the death of Wolcott Balestier and the outbreak of flu that kept a number of relations away.

'That woman [a most derogatory expression in those days] is going to marry our Ruddy.' It would be interesting to know exactly what John meant by his comment, 'Carrie Balestier was a good man spoiled.' When the marriage came, Henry James, who gave away the bride, wrote to his brother William, 'She is a hard devoted capable little person whom I don't in the least understand his marrying.' That sort of thing is often said about couples who turn out to be well matched, and some might mutter that to mystify James over some piece of normal human behaviour was no great feat.

But that stage was not reached for over a year. What happened between the couple in the meantime, except that they continued to meet, is undiscoverable. Even the admirably detailed biography by Charles Carrington says of the courtship only that 'it did not run smoothly,' a remark based on 'personal information'. It would, again, be well worth knowing which of the two put up the more opposition, or rather to have one's suspicions confirmed.

Kipling was ill that winter with tropical diseases contracted in India. A long sea-voyage was recommended. After some vacillation, he set off alone on a trip round the world in August 1891. His chief ports of call were in the White Dominions: South Africa, New Zealand and Australia, though he did not stay long in any. Late in the year he landed in Ceylon (Sri Lanka) and soon took the train up through India to Lahore. He was with his parents when a cable arrived from Carrie: Wolcott Balestier was dead of typhoid in Germany. Kipling left at once, not staying for Christmas as he had

Colombo harbour, Ceylon (Sri Lanka), 1880s. Kipling struck up an acquaintance with General William Booth, founder of the Salvation Army, on the way from Australia.

planned. On 10 January he was back in London and on the 18th he and Carrie were married. The speed of all this has led commentators to conclude that the couple 'must have' been engaged, or nearly engaged, before Kipling left on his travels; the only actual evidence lies in another item of personal information supplied to Professor Carrington. It is quite unspecified and so cannot be evaluated.

There is nothing odd or surprising about any of this. Grief for Wolcott swept away whatever resistance to the match there might have been. The blow certainly hit Kipling hard, hard enough to damage his literary judgment. When *Barrack-Room Ballads* appeared as a book, he commemorated his dead friend in a dedicatory poem that was triply embarrassing: part of it was based on an earlier poem about something else, its language would seem rather high-flown even if applied to St Francis or Nelson, and what on earth had Wolcott Balestier to do with Tommy Atkins? Nevertheless, the poem is touching as a gesture.

The marriage (to round off the topic) was as happy as most. In some respects, Carrie was the dominant partner. She organized her husband's affairs, kept his accounts, saw to his mail, filtered his visitors – a useful service for a man who hated intrusion and who was so much sought after. Several observers, perhaps expecting him to show at home the fire-breathing quality they had read into parts of his work, thought she overdid her superintendence, but much of it suited Kipling. Some men like being protected, even mothered a little, without being the less manly for it.

Their daughter Elsie, later Mrs George Bambridge, has written what seems a remarkably fair-minded account of her parents' relationship. Her mother was moody and difficult, often filling those round her with her own tensions: a not unfamiliar type. This attribute sometimes exhausted Kipling, though he never complained. On the other hand, Carrie was intelligent, witty, loyal, kind, and above all brave. Mrs Bambridge concludes:

My father's much exaggerated reputation as a recluse sprang, to a certain extent, from her domination of his life and the way in which she tried to shelter him from the world. To a certain degree this was a good thing and enabled him to work without too much interruption, but he needed also the stimulus of good talk and mixing with people, and as the years went on and his life became more restricted, he missed these keenly.

Kipling's money troubles were over for the time being. He and Carrie would go on a real trip round the world. They reached New York in February 1892 and as soon as possible left that 'grotesquely bad' place to visit Carrie's family near Brattleboro in Vermont. Kipling – or was it Carrie? – decided they must settle here on the family estate in due course. Some land was made over to them by her brother Beatty Balestier, an amiable scapegrace. With this agreed, the couple

Book-plate designed by John Lockwood Kipling for his granddaughter Elsie.

travelled to the west coast of the continent, partly by way of Canada, a country for which Kipling always had a particular affection. In the spring they came to Japan, which he found less attractive than three years previously; his mistrust of its system was sharpened. Some such forebodings proved well founded when most of his money vanished in the closedown of a bank. They had to make a prompt return to Brattleboro.

For a year they lived modestly in a small cottage on the estate. It was there that, in December, their first child, Josephine, was born. The following spring, their financial worries now over for good, they set about having a house built to their own plan: this included an arrangement whereby it was impossible to get to Kipling's study except past Carrie's desk. The place was christened Naulakha* in memory of Wolcott and the family moved in at the end of the summer. For the next three years it was their base, though there were trips to Bermuda and to England, an enforced stay in Washington for Carrie's recovery from a domestic accident, and Kipling visited Gloucester, Mass., to look at the fishing-fleet (a source of material for *Captains Courageous*). Elsie was born in February 1896.

Until the last few months, their stay in Vermont was a contented and useful one. Kipling worked hard; he was so settled that American naturalization seemed possible. (If it had come to pass, would anyone like to guess when the USA would have entered the First World War?) Then, two disparate series of events combined to upset fatally the ordered life at Naulakha.

The Bliss Cottage, Brattleboro, Vermont: the Kiplings' first home. 'My workroom in the Bliss Cottage was seven feet by eight, and from December to April the snow lay level with its window-sill.'

* The correct spelling: Wolcott had got it wrong in the novel. Why Kipling never put him right is a mystery.

Main Street, Brattleboro, *c.* 1890.
The Kiplings sometimes stayed in
the building with the balcony, the
town's principal hotel.

'Mr Kipling did not like to have his
picture taken', declared John R.
Bliss, but 'one of the boys got in the
peanut stand and snapped this
picture' in Main Street, 1893.

'Building "Naulakha" gave us both
a life-long taste for playing with
timber, stone, concrete and such
delightful things', Kipling recalled
in *Something of Myself*.

'Kipling at the wheelbarrow', a
picture drawn by the staff artist of
The Boston Globe from a clandestine
snapshot, 1893.

View of Brattleboro from the Bliss Farm: shared by Kipling in 1892–93 as he wrote the *Jungle Book* stories.

In 1895 the States and England had fallen out over a frontier dispute in South America. Hostility continued for months, war was supposed possible at one stage, and although matters were patched up in mid-1896, Kipling's confidence in his position in the US was badly damaged. He also became involved in a family quarrel. Beatty Balestier had quarrelled with his sister, among other things over their respective rights to part of the land round Naulakha. He had gone bankrupt and was drinking with some persistence. He may have resented his brother-in-law's affluence and fame: anyway, there was a scene that stopped short of fisticuffs but went as far as Beatty threatening Kipling's life. Whether it was a serious threat or not, Kipling went to the police. Beatty was arrested. There was immense and, to Kipling at any rate, agonizing publicity. Before the trial could take place, the Kiplings had left for England.

A possible third factor in this move was loneliness. Visitors were frequent at Naulakha, but Kipling had made few local friends and the house was physically cut off – at his choice, but not necessarily to his eventual liking. In his autobiography, he tells of the visit he made, it seems on the spur of the moment, to the only house in sight from his own. The woman who came to the door said, 'Be you the new lights 'crost the valley yonder? Ye don't know what a comfort they've been to me this winter. Ye ain't ever going to shroud 'em up – or *be* ye?' (He never did.) Nor much pondering is needed in order to see the implications of this anecdote. Kipling was rediscovering 'the dread meaning of loneliness' in full. And there was nothing there to write about, a severe deprivation for one so dependent on his surroundings for subject-matter. He produced a single story with a Vermont setting, 'A Walking Delegate', in which the characters are horses.

As already noted, the Vermont years were productive – of stories and poems founded on previous experience. Their quality is uneven.

The Jungle Book and *The Second Jungle Book* were once enormously popular with children, and even today not many people need to be told who Mowgli and Shere Khan are, though this knowledge must sometimes come only from having seen the Disney film. The judgment of an adult in such cases is not worth much; I can say little more than that I remember not liking them in my childhood. If memory serves, what put me off was something I would now try to define as paraded wisdom. I may have sensed what must be true, that they are very much the sort of books adults give children. Perhaps there ought to be an 'it might seem' before the 'enormously popular' above.*

The stories collected in *Many Inventions*, some of which had been written or begun in London, include an excellent piece of straight science fiction in 'A Matter of Fact' (it ends with a dig at the United States), and an enjoyable action yarn about southern Africa, 'Judson and the Empire'. Two others are of higher repute without (some readers may think) altogether deserving it.

'"The Finest Story in the World"' is a story about a story that never gets written because the man with the material for it, a London clerk who remembers previous existences as a galley-slave, keeps turning his attention to what he thinks are more important matters. So they are: the unwritten story, from what we are told of it, could never have come anywhere near being the finest in the world, because

'"He is afraid of me," said little Toomai, and he made Kala Nag lift up his feet one after the other.' From the first edition of *The Jungle Book*, 1894.

* When, in 1893–94, some of the *Jungle Book* stories were published in *St Nicholas*, a leading US juvenile magazine, the normally vocal readership was silent. Not a single communication about them or their author reached its popular 'Letter Box' feature. As against this implied view, let me quote a six-year-old British commentator of our own day, who writes: 'I like [these] stories because they have a lot of action. They're very exciting and they're funny. [Kipling] writes things that sound a bit truish really.'

the details about the galleys, though they seem most convincing, are not of great interest in themselves, and the written story fails because reincarnation is such an intractably dull idea.

In '"Love-o'-Women"', what is between the inner pair of quotes is supposed to be a man's nickname. This excites incredulity: could you bring yourself to say, for instance, 'Have one on me, Love-o'-Women'? Kipling here indulges too in his favourite vice of over-mystification – old Love-o'-Women is a disappointed man, but we never find out quite what disappointed him. The climax, though melodramatic and improbable, touches our pity, and the opening is admittedly splendid, perhaps the most powerful he ever devised (see p. 114). It turns out, however, to be the opening to one of his frame-narratives.

The poems of the American period likewise vary in merit. There were more Barrack-Room Ballads, almost up to the level of the original series. Kipling was breaking fresh ground as well in pieces like 'The Song of the Banjo', which would be among his very finest achievements but for its idiotic choruses. The most celebrated

Kipling's home at Rottingdean. The Burne-Joneses had a house in the village, as did the Ridsdales, whose daughter, Cissie, married Stanley Baldwin.

of the new poems are the two long, elaborate dramatic monologues, 'M'Andrew's Hymn' and 'The "Mary Gloster"'. They are certainly fine performances, technically outstanding even for their author, but some readers (here they are again) have found in them more to admire than to be moved by.

The four Kiplings arrived back in England in September 1896 and first took a house near Torquay, then settled in the village of Rotting-dean, near Brighton. There was no shortage of companionship now, and none of public attention, either. Kipling was becoming more than a leading writer with an unusually large audience (large enough to warrant the issue of a uniform edition of his works when he was still in his early thirties): he soon turned into a national figure. This was partly the result of his having begun to contribute to *The Times* a number of poems on important issues of the day.

These pieces are not patriotic; they take patriotism for granted. Their subject is not the greatness of England but her duties and dangers. The tone is grave and quiet: again he had found a new style for a new

German efficiency may have brought
order out of jungle chaos in Africa –
as the Munich *Jugend* (1896) suggests
– but for Kipling its connection with
nationalist aggression was to be
deplored.

theme. 'Recessional' is the best known and one of the best, an urgent
warning against the irresponsible use of national power written on the
occasion of Queen Victoria's Golden Jubilee in 1897. One phrase
in it, 'lesser breeds without the Law', is still liable to be misunderstood.
The reference is not to Indians or any other Asians, none at that time
being any sort of international threat, but to European nationalisms,
chiefly German, as Orwell pointed out in his essay of 1942. These
are without the Law of duty and self-restraint (see p. 55) in that they
do not recognize it. Another phrase in another fine poem, '" For All
We Have and Are"' (1914), brought Kipling some obloquy. 'The
Hun is at the gate' has been taken as an incitement to racial hatred.
No: 'the Hun' is a metaphor for 'the barbarian, the enemy of decent

values', and 'the gate' is not that of England and the Empire, but that of civilization. If there is a fault here, it is one of overstatement only.

This series of poems made Kipling the national bard in place of Tennyson, who had died in 1892 after over forty years as Poet Laureate. The office had been filled again in 1896 by the nonentity Alfred Austin; Kipling, though strongly lobbied for, had not even been approached, on the grounds that he would certainly have refused. (When Austin died in 1913, the situation repeated itself.) In time, Kipling was to turn down a knighthood and other titles, while accepting honorary degrees and, in 1907, the Nobel Prize for Literature. Recognition by a government meant recognition by a political party, and no political party must feel that it had reason to count on his support. He had to retain his freedom of action. Very well, but why did he also decline the Order of Merit? This was in the gift not of Lloyd George or Stanley Baldwin, but of King George V, with whom Kipling was on warm personal terms by the time of the last offer. I cannot explain this.

At first sight, Kipling's attitude to public recognition is not altogether straightforward. He had a 'horror' of intrusions on his personal life, of reporters, of the regular bus-loads of sightseers who came peering into his garden at Rottingdean, even into his house. This feeling was so strong in him that in one of his science-fiction stories, 'As Easy as ABC', he went so far as to depict a future state of society in which invasion of privacy is a uniquely serious legal offence. At the same time he joined clubs, went in for speech-making, gave readings from his works and, considering his profession, could not have gone a better way about becoming a public figure if he had tried. This hardly seems to indicate a *horror* of being brought up against strangers. 'Dislike' is acceptable, and preferring to meet people on one's own terms is common and natural.

Kipling arrived in Stockholm to receive the Nobel Prize to find the city in mourning for the death of the King of Sweden.

Kipling (in the foreground, with his face partly obscured by Mark Twain's academic cap) receives an honorary degree in Oxford, 27 June 1907.

79

The period 1897–1902 produced its full share of prose. First to be published was *Captains Courageous*, a short novel more popular, according to Carrington, with American than British readers. The details of maritime life have their own interest, but the plot is defective. There is not a single first-rate story in the collection called *The Day's Work*: some scrapings of the Indian barrel, a couple of half-cock Anglo-American jokes, some accounts of personified machinery and of personified animals which must be of limited appeal.

Captains Courageous: the attempt to portray the virtues of plain fishermen in contrast to the corruption of the American Gilded Age was not a success.

One of the machinery stories, '.007', concerns an American railway engine. An American railwayman complained that it was full of inaccuracies: 'if [Kipling] had spent a night in a roundhouse [engine-shed] with his ears open he would never have used "loco" for locomotive'; he would not have said 'bogie' when he meant 'truck', put the parlour-car in the wrong place, painted the engine the wrong colour, etc. It does seem that writers noted for authenticity constantly trip up in this way; even I, with my tiny knowledge of both fields, can catch Kipling out on the bull-fight and on naval gunnery. He is wrong about the manufacture of liqueurs, too. This kind of misfortune also afflicted the late Ian Fleming, who turns up naturally enough in a .007 context.

Stalky & Co., mentioned earlier, aroused some opposition when it appeared. An eloquent and unintentionally very funny attack came from one Robert Buchanan, a now-forgotten novelist and controversialist who had earlier denounced the Pre-Raphaelite poets for the naked eroticism of their work. 'Only the spoiled child of an utterly brutalised public could possibly have written "Stalky & Co."', he screamed now, went on about 'horrible vileness', and thought the central trio 'not like boys at all, but like hideous little men'. That last remark is nearer the bone. Boyishness is missing from the book, and with it departs some probability, and with that we lose some interest too. The trouble with the various adventures is

The railway station, Brattleboro, *c.* 1894, where the baggage master recalled that Kipling 'would sit and listen and never stir . . . I never saw a man so hungry for information.' But the listening and the hunger did not guarantee accuracy.

Rudyard's own drawing of 'The Elephant's Child' from the first edition of the *Just So Stories*, 1902.

not that they are revenge-fantasies, or that they are 'vile', but that they are rather dull. And Stalky and the others are not particularly hideous, but they are not very attractive either. They lack warmth.

This adult thinks, for what it is worth, that the *Just So Stories: for little children* would be just the thing for little children, who seem to agree. The book has not gone the way of the *Jungle Books*: it is still very much read, or read out of to. The illustrations by the author are of great interest to those with any sort of interest in him. They are highly competent, often haunting, often comic, and always (of

Kim and the
letter-writer

John Lockwood Kipling illustrated
the first edition of *Kim*, 1901.

course) marked by a strong personal outlook. An artist of some merit
was lost in Kipling, or rather declared redundant while his *alter ego*
forged on with the pen.

Kim (1901) is the crown of this period and quite likely of Kipling's
whole output, in prose at least. Late in life, he lamented that he had
never written a real novel; *Kim* did not count; it was 'nakedly
picaresque and plotless'. What of that? It is a narrative with characters
and events; it is not only the finest story about India (Chaudhuri's
verdict), but one of the greatest novels in the language. Its subject is

the land and the people. Kipling's gift for accumulating detail was never shown better or at such length or with such power: sights, sounds, smells and exactly what men and women wear, exactly what they do in the course of their travels and of settling down for the night, exactly what they eat and how they cook and serve every dish – and if he says coriander when he means cardamum I will let it go. The people are shown not just in the mass, but in four carefully varied individual portraits: a Pathan, an elderly upper-caste lady from the North-West Provinces, a Bengali, and a Tibetan lama. These, especially the last, are triumphs of educated imagination. There is nothing like them anywhere else, not even in the rest of Kipling's work. And he wished he had written something 'worthy to lie alongside *The Cloister and the Hearth*', Charles Reade's tattered bolt of pseudo-medieval fustian!

In January 1898 the Kiplings took ship for Cape Town. They were now five in number, a son having been born the previous August; he was christened John after his grandfather. The purposes of the journey were to avoid the English winter, chiefly for the sake of Kipling's health, and to give him a second look at South Africa for interest's sake. As it turned out, the visit was to mark the beginning of an important episode in his life. He renewed an acquaintance with Alfred Milner, the British High Commissioner, and Cecil Rhodes, the founder of the recently named colony of Rhodesia (which in those days included what is now Zambia). Kipling took the train up to Bulawayo and explored it on a bicycle. He also studied the

Kipling met Rhodes with Milner in London after his election to the Athenaeum. Rhodes later built him a house on his estate in Cape Town, and Kipling wintered there, 1900–07. Here Rhodes is seen in 1897, to the left of centre in the photograph.

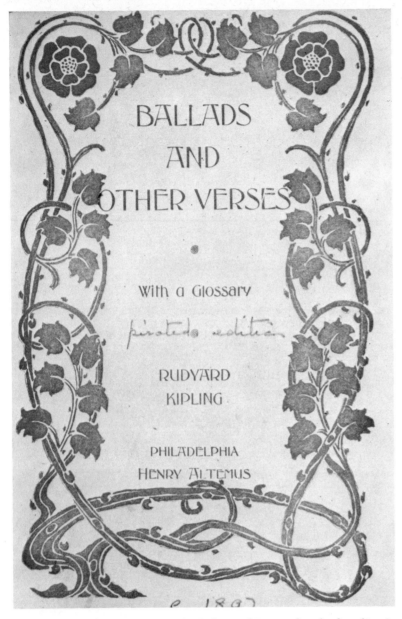

BALLADS
AND
OTHER VERSES

·

With a Glossary

pirated edition

RUDYARD
KIPLING

PHILADELPHIA
HENRY ALTEMUS

1897

Copyright problems in America: one of the unauthorized editions of Kipling's work.

conditions under which the English-speaking settlers had to live in the two Boer republics of the Transvaal and the Orange Free State, and found them abominable. When he left in April he was already a convinced though not violent anti-Boer.

The projected 1898–99 winter trip was cancelled in favour of one to the United States: Carrie wanted to see her mother and Kipling had some copyright trouble to clear up; not perhaps a very pressing motive in his case. The Atlantic crossing was rough. Josephine and

The famous portrait of Kipling by Sir Philip Burne-Jones, 1899.

Elsie caught colds; on arrival in New York their condition worsened, then improved again. Carrie, too, came down with fever; she soon recovered. But the sickness would not go away. Kipling was soon taken seriously ill with pneumonia, so much so that his life was feared for. Crowds gathered outside his hotel, and it can be said as truly as it can ever be said that the world waited anxiously for the outcome. As the reader will know, it was favourable in his case. Six-year-old Josephine, however, had suffered a relapse and died a couple of days after her father was pronounced out of danger.

It took Kipling months to recover from his illness: nothing is known of his recovery from the loss of his daughter. As soon as he could travel, in June 1899, he took the remnants of his family back to England. He never again visited the United States.

That October, the South African War broke out. I cannot set forth its rights and wrongs here, or perhaps anywhere. It is enough that Kipling took the British side, partly, like his friends Milner and

Opposite, Josephine Kipling: 'the daughter that was all to him'.

Above, the Royal Canadian
Regiment and the 1st Gordon
Highlanders fording the Modder
River in February 1900 during the
Boer War.

Kipling with other war
correspondents at Glover's Island,
c. 1900.

Truth's Christmas prediction, 1900, of the scene at Paardeburg seven years later.

Rhodes, out of instinct, partly, again like them, because he felt he had seen evidence that the Boers were enemies of freedom and progress in that part of the world. At any rate, he worked for the cause. He formed a volunteer company at Rottingdean; he drummed up money for soldiers' dependants; he wrote poems. The first of these, 'The Absent-Minded Beggar', was also used as a fund-raiser: reprint fees, performing rights and the like brought in £250,000.

In all, Kipling spent seven or eight months of the next two and a half years in South Africa. He visited wounded, worked for an Army newspaper, was closely consulted by generals and politicians, had a ringside view of a battle. He saw the workings of the Empire more intimately, and when they were under much greater stress, than ever during his time in India. And yet all that came directly out of this contact, which continued in peacetime, was three second-rate stories and some ephemeral verses. Perhaps he had not cared for the experience; especially in its first months, the war had shown up England as less strong than might have been thought. It seems clear that the patriotic zeal he had shown in those first months diminished later. The book he completed at Cape Town in early 1902 was his *Just So Stories*.

The year 1902 was one of change for Kipling. Peace was signed in South Africa. Kipling and his family moved into their final house, Bateman's, at Burwash in Sussex. Half his life was over, the more important half in many ways. When Orwell said of Kipling that

'Yes, it's all our own including a mill which was paying taxes in 1296!' Kipling was pleased with his new home at Bateman's.

90

he 'belongs very definitely to the period 1885–1902', he had in mind Kipling's political outlook, his seeming failure to accommodate himself to subsequent changes in that sphere. No doubt, but his best work belongs there as definitely. There have been recent attempts to uncover neglected merit in the writings of the 'mature' (i.e. later) years, especially in the stories, and indeed there are some splendid pieces there. All the same, it would never do to try to exalt those writings into anything like a balance with what had gone before. Kipling developed early and he went off early.

It is an often-indulged temptation to see a link between an artist's immediate environment and what he produces in it. Such a link cannot be simple or in any way decisive. Nevertheless, those who find a brooding, dejected, withdrawn or hemmed-in quality in parts of the 'mature' Kipling might care for a note or two on a visit I made to Bateman's early in 1973.

I went in the mundane, busy company of a television unit to make a short film in a series about writers and their houses. Bateman's, set apart from the small village which is itself miles from any town, lies in a watery hollow, but looked attractive enough with the winter sunshine on its Jacobean grey stone. Inside, it was quite different:

Bateman's was to be Kipling's home for thirty-four years, until his death in 1936.

Bateman's: the front door (*right*), the entrance hall (*opposite above*) and Kipling's study (*opposite below*).

chilly, damp, and dark even on the south side. Houses in themselves are of course as insignificant as any other objects, and cannot by their nature possess an 'atmosphere'; even so, I soon decided that I should very much dislike spending as much as twenty-four hours in that one. Of my colleagues, all those I spoke to about it agreed with me, a couple of them volunteering the view.

One of the best stories Kipling wrote after settling in Bateman's is 'The House Surgeon', a powerful macabre tale about a house that throws a pall of depression over occupants and visitors. This is supposed to refer to his house near Torquay, in which both he and Carrie are known to have felt uncomfortable. I suggest that if he had ever needed a refresher course in such feelings he had only to go into his own tenebrous, low-ceilinged study on the first floor at Bateman's. 'The House Surgeon', by the way, could not have been written earlier than 1904, seven years after he left Torquay.

MEN of different trades and sizes
Here you see before your eyeses;
Lanky sword and stumpy pen,
Doing useful things for men;
When the Empire wants a stitch in her
Send for Kipling and for Kitchener.

Illustration by F. Carruthers Gould
from *The Struwwelpeter Alphabet*,
1908.

It would be unfair, and false too, to conclude that Kipling spent
his last thirty-four years in an overground dungeon.* He was one of
the first motorists, beginning with a steam-driven American 'loco-
mobile' in which he explored Sussex. He and Carrie went on visits
and received visitors, from Stephen Leacock to Georges Clemenceau,
though they saw few of their neighbours. The South African trips
ceased after 1908. Developments there had disappointed Kipling, who

* My poem, 'Kipling at Bateman's', suggests that none the less there were elements of that –
suggests only, not concludes. A poem cannot conclude anything.

had not bargained for seeing, within a few years of England's dearly won victory, preparations under way for a Union of South Africa – under the British Crown, admittedly, but according equal rights to the Boers, who were the wrong 'race' (letter of 1901) to do any governing. But in 1907 there had been a visit to his beloved Canada, and in 1909–14 the family took winter holidays on the Continent, chiefly in France, a country to which he always showed a very unjingoistic devotion. In 1913 they went as far as Egypt, where Lord Kitchener proved to be engaged in maladministration. The half-dozen years before the First World War found Kipling engaged in speech-making – not written propaganda – on behalf of the right wing of the Conservative Party.

One of the most famous (by name at any rate) of Kipling's volumes is *Puck of Pook's Hill* (1906), a linked series of tales told in the first person by characters from selected stages of our island story, of whom the best presented is a Roman centurion. Always one to fiddle with modes of presentation, Kipling has each of them in turn summoned in the flesh by the not unamiable sprite, Puck, for the benefit of two comparatively unrevolting Edwardian children – it is a children's book that has won much favour from adults. The structure has its drawbacks. There are constant interruptions at which questions are asked and hard bits cleared up. This helps to see to it that what should be romantic becomes businesslike and everyday. As Gillian Avery has acutely observed, the various narrators 'are not ghosts, there is no nimbus of mystery about them, and they seemed to me as a child like dressed-up figures from a pageant'. Puck would have been better advised to turn his time-machine round and send the children off to the past with no one to hold their hands. The tales themselves are often clever and vivid, but they are weighed down by the sense that the author's grasp of the sweep of British history is being not so much drawn upon as shown off.

The two collections of stories, *Traffics and Discoveries* and *Actions and Reactions*, can be considered together: both are mixed bags. At the top of the list come three tales of the supernatural, not the savage or horrific supernatural as we meet it in some of the Indian pieces, but something gentle and elegiac. 'The House Surgeon', just referred to, is remarkable not only for its evocations of malaise but also for, so to speak, the clarity of its mystery: the reason for the haunting and the manner of its dispersal are conveyed in full without a word of overt explanation. '"Wireless"' is better known, but it cuts less deep. The reader's attention is directed more to the skilful counterpointing of its two themes – communication in space by telegraphy and in time by some means or other – than to the pathos of the consumptive chemist's-assistant whose mind becomes attuned to that of Keats.

In another famous tale, 'They', a character seeming to represent Kipling comes across a Sussex house and garden in which a blind woman is surrounded by the ghosts of dead children, one of whom proves near the end to be the visitor's daughter. It is perhaps the directness of the link between the later part of the story and Kipling's loss of Josephine that has led critics to conclude that that loss has not been fully 'resolved into art' (Bonamy Dobrée). This sort of complaint does damage to 'Baa, Baa, Black Sheep' but not, I think, to 'They'. If we did not know what we know, we might conclude from it only that its author had understood a large part of what parents feel about their children. An (understandably) easy focus for sentimentality need not be sentimental in itself.

There are three other notable, or noted, stories in these two collections. 'With the Night Mail' is an interesting piece of science fiction, ahead of its time in more than the obvious sense with its enthusiastic delineation of a non-existent technology. The use of feigned magazine extracts, including facsimile advertisements, is deeply science-fictional, a commendation I need not explain to those who know the genre, and cannot in this space to those who do not. As is the way with such matters, 'Mrs Bathurst' has by its obscurity attracted attention instead of repelling it; authorial self-indulgence can leave out too much as well as put too much in (see p. 106). A discussion of the third of these three, 'An Habitation Enforced', is deferred for the moment.

Rewards and Fairies, a sequel to *Puck of Pook's Hill*, turns out to contain that deservedly celebrated poem, 'The Way through the Woods', a pastoral lyric so well done and so far outside its author's usual range, whatever that is, as to make it difficult to think of a literary parallel; Verdi's String Quartet might furnish a rough musical one. Two other poems of the years leading up to the First World War stand out from a large mass of the second-rate, not that second-rate Kipling is to be despised. 'The Wage-Slaves' sums up his creed of the dignity of work in tones of sober emphasis with an ironical edge and a poise that falters only in the last four lines. 'The Sons of Martha' takes the same theme at a quicker pace, mingling the literal and the figurative with triumphant ease until, again, the end, which brings a sad lurch into religiosity.

Some of that second-rate verse yields something to the biographer's lens. A poem like 'Sussex', in which the natural and man-made beauties of the county are hymned, is well written, observant, thoughtful and too emphatic, the work of a man pushing down his roots by will-power. The same could be said of the story, 'An Habitation Enforced', in which an American couple settle among English country-folk. The latter are too wise and understanding and un-

Kipling as a war correspondent in France.

changed and selfless by half. Nobody shows the strangers any hostility, suspicion or even indifference. Some scenes could even form the basis of the script of a heart-warming American film starring Robert Taylor and Sylvia Sidney. To put the matter less colourfully, the tone and content of the story are Anglophile, something which a real Englishman cannot be.

This failure of connection was soon spotted, among others by G. K. Chesterton, who wrote of Kipling that he was 'the globe-trotter; he has not the patience to become part of anything'. And so 'he thinks of England as a place': we do not think of our home as, or primarily as, a place. Chesterton could hardly have known that, only a year or so before 'Sussex' was published, Kipling had written in a letter to Rhodes: 'England is a stuffy little place, mentally, morally and physically.' Not long after Kipling's death, over thirty years later, T. S. Eliot commented on his 'detachment and remoteness from all environment. . . . He remains somehow [yes, but how?] alien and aloof from all with which he identifies himself.'

On the information available to each, Chesterton was right and Eliot wrong. Kipling may have put down his roots on purpose, but eventually they struck. Two rather later stories suggest this. '"My Son's Wife"' (1913) is a gentle, mildly funny rustic comedy in which we can detect a full and genuine assimilation of Sussex and England, and 'Friendly Brook' (1914), while insisting firmly on its author's understanding of the rural life about him, does so only in so far as it is his *métier* to understand people unlike himself, with no more emphasis than can be found in *Kim*. After spending most of his youth abroad or in transit, Kipling had managed to make himself into an Englishman who thought of England as home.

The war that Kipling had foreseen and feared came about. To him, what England had undertaken was a defensive crusade, the acceptance of a terrible necessity. No one could have been less subject to dreams of any simple triumph.

He and Carrie got down to practical work on behalf of Belgian refugees and with the Red Cross. Although troubled by illness, he engaged upon a round of military hospitals and camps in England, then, in August 1915, a visit to the troops in France that took him to the front line. In the following month he visited ships of the Royal Navy at official request. A few days after his return to Bateman's, there arrived a telegram with the news that his son John, aged just eighteen and serving as a subaltern with the Irish Guards, was wounded and missing in France.

Kipling, experienced in such matters, knew at once what this signified. According to one account, Lord Beaverbrook (then Max Aitken) arrived at the house for lunch that very day and was met

outside it by his host, who told him that John was dead; Beaverbrook turned his car round and drove back to London. It was over two years before that death and its gallant circumstances were finally established, though the body was never found. Kipling surmounted the loss with remarkable bravery and reticence. In the official history of the Irish Guards which he began to work on in 1917, his son appears only as a name on a casualty list.

Kipling had little time to write fiction during the war. Two stories of early 1915, however, are of particular interest. The dating is important:

immediately beforehand, England had suffered her first air-raids, with more and far worse expected; the U-boat campaign against merchant shipping was officially announced; and reports of German atrocities in Belgium had been circulated – true or not, they were widely believed.

The first-begun of these stories, 'Sea-Constables', tells how a British captain refused medical aid to the captain of a neutral ship that had been trading with the Germans, whereupon the man died. The author makes no explicit comment, but the message is clear: serve him right! This disagreeable tale is presented in Kipling's most irritating style, virtually all in dialogue crammed with technicalities and leaving obscure what exactly took place. He did not have the story printed in book form until 1926, which perhaps suggests that he had his own doubts about it.

'Mary Postgate' is a different matter (it was collected in 1917). Mary is a middle-aged virgin, companion to an infirm old lady. One day a bomb falls on their village and kills a little girl. Soon afterwards, Mary finds a mortally hurt German airman lying in the shrubbery. So far from calling a doctor, she fetches a revolver and brandishes it at the injured man, saying in broken German that she has seen the dead child. Within minutes the airman dies, at which point Mary experiences sexual release. That is the crux; there are other things in the story, including a couple of obscurities: why and where the aeroplane crashed, for instance.

It was Kipling's not very rewarding habit to preface and follow his stories with short poems. These can usually be skipped and read out of context in the collected verse. Not this time: 'Mary Postgate' has for suffix 'The Beginnings', which is literally a hymn of hate, and it does not just happen to be there as part of a kind of micro-anthology of pieces relating to the war. No: its presence means, I am afraid, that the message of the story – Kipling would certainly have said that he dealt in messages – is not something like, 'Well, what would you expect in the circumstances?', but, again, 'Serve him right!' We could pass over the whole business in embarrassed silence if 'Mary Postgate' were not one of its author's finest performances, as penetrating a character-study as he ever achieved. It must continue to trouble his admirers and fortify his detractors. (He had beyond doubt begun it more than six months before he learned that his son was missing.)

A great deal of the wartime verse is, not surprisingly, occasional, called forth by some turn in affairs abroad or at home. In large part it survives as poetry long after its demise as propaganda. General statements of defiance like 'A Song in Storm' retain their impact; elegies like 'The Children' still go to the heart; the indignation of 'Mesopotamia' will touch those who never knew its cause; 'Mine-

Opposite above, Rider Haggard: 'A long talk with Kipling is now one of the greatest pleasures I have left in life', he wrote in 1918.

Opposite below, Rudyard and Carrie Kipling at the cemetery in Loos, scene of the battle in which their son John was killed in 1915.

Sweepers', with its extraordinary verse-movement, is as fresh as ever. What a librettist he would have made – how well, as it is, his lyrics go to music! Did Elgar never think of approaching him?

After the war, Kipling's ill-health continued. Carrie was more protective than ever: she even came to supervise the farming of the estate. But there were constant visitors, from Rider Haggard to Frank Buchman, and Kipling kept in touch with technological developments, especially aeronautical ones. When, in 1919, the airship *R.34* crossed the Atlantic, the crew took with them one book, his *Traffics and Discoveries*, to compare their experience with the science-fiction airship story in it, 'With the Night Mail'. The volume was finally presented to him autographed by everyone on board. Such was the nature and extent of his fame.

The Kiplings continued to travel, especially to France. The first few of these visits were hardly pleasure-trips. They involved Kipling, now a member of the Imperial War Graves Commission, in inspecting and reporting on the state of the British and Dominion burial-grounds. On one of these tours, in 1922, he was presented to King

BRAZILIAN SKETCHES

ADAM AND THE SERPENT

VISIT TO A MODERN SNAKE FARM

BY

RUDYARD KIPLING

"Poison of asps is under our lips"?
  Why do you seek us then?
Breaking our knotted fellow-ships
  With your noisy-footed men?

Time and time over we let them go;
  Hearing and slipping aside;
Until they followed and troubled us—so
  We struck back, and they died.

" Poison of asps is under our lips "?
  Why do you wrench them apart,—
To learn how the venom makes and drips
  And works its way to the heart.

It is unjust that when we have done
  All that a serpent should,
You gather our poisons, one by one,
  And break them down to your good.

" Poison of asps is under our lips."
  That is your answer? No!
Because we hissed at Adam's eclipse
  Is the reason you hate us so.

George V, there on an official occasion; it was from that encounter that their friendship sprang up. After another and more serious bout of illness in the same year, Kipling was on the move again, to the Continent, to North Africa, to Brazil, and in 1930 to the West Indies, the Kiplings' last long voyage.

Politically he became more and more isolated, falling off the right wing of the Conservative Party. Perhaps I should repeat here that such a position had nothing to do with fascism. When he found out what Hitler was up to he ceased his lifelong habit of marking his books with the Hindu good-luck emblem of the swastika (a mirror-image of the Nazi one), and in his last public speech he gave a warning of Germany's aggressive intentions. There was almost no one in power he felt he could rely on except the King, who shared some of his knowledge of the Empire and his concern for what was happening in it. He no longer trusted his cousin Baldwin, Tory Prime Minister through a large part of the 1920s, growling, 'Stanley is a Socialist at heart.'

His literary standing was curious. The critics who had discovered and praised him had shifted their enthusiasm to newer luminaries. On the other side of the spectrum lay the Kipling Society (founded 1927), whose hagiographical activities he regarded with 'gloomy distaste' – Carrington's phrase. In the middle was the great mass of readers all over the world. He went on writing, but he would have done that even if nobody had been paying attention.

Kipling's penultimate collection of stories, *Debits and Credits*, appeared in 1926. It contains some self-indulgent fantasy, some exercises in the supernatural, evidence of a preoccupation with disease, some stuff about Freemasons, and three good stories. There is more good than that in the volume: it is hard to find anything by Kipling that is without its successful moments.

In 'The Wish House', the interests in the supernatural and in disease are combined. An old countrywoman has intentionally visited on herself the cancer once suffered by her former lover. This part is done with assured restraint, but what is more striking is the skill and insight with which the old woman is made to reveal her nature, her history, her ways of thought to a sympathetic contemporary. Kipling, at sixty-odd, is extending his range once more.

The same combination of themes is to be found in 'A Madonna of the Trenches'. Here perhaps there is some superfluity. For the phantom of a woman in England to appear to her lover in wartime France is all right (better, in fact), and the same can be said of her mysterious ability to foresee the exact date of her death from cancer. The two together form a largeish lump to swallow, and the Masonic frame-story does not help to wash it down.

Opposite, he continued to use his experiences – here, on his visit to Brazil – to produce poems and other pieces for newspapers and magazines. From *The Morning Post*, 9 December 1927.

103

Opposite, centre of attention at a
garden party: the British Embassy,
Paris, July 1931.

'The Eye of Allah' is a kind of science fiction. A forerunner of the
microscope turns up in a thirteenth-century English monastery and
is destroyed on purpose as too likely to attract charges of diabolism.
The monastic setting displays Kipling's grasp of detail – detail of
processes as well as of appearances – at its very best.

The last collection, *Limits and Renewals* (1932), shows a sad but not
strange decline. Disease, now accompanied by madness, comes back
as a recurrent theme. There is a revenge-comedy, 'Beauty Spots',
among Kipling's unfunniest, which is saying something. There is a
neat detective story in 'Fairy-Kist', despite its title. And, among
other pieces, there is 'Dayspring Mishandled', which seems to
Professor J. M. S. Tompkins, usually an excellent critic, 'one of
Kipling's great achievements'. I think that to consider it so is to consider too curiously. She (the Professor) rightly draws attention to the
masterly way in which it is presented, but the author has too obviously
set out to win such praise, and what is presented, the tale of a literary
forgery got up by one scholar to deceive and so ruin another, is surely a
squalid revenge-tragedy, not redeemed by the forger's eventual
recognition of its squalor. His motive is bedimmed by a mystification
near the outset, and from what we are shown of the text of the forged
document, a supposed fragment of Chaucer, the deception thereby
of an acknowledged expert is not altogether probable.

One of the disease-and-madness group has prefixed to it a poem,
'Hymn to Physical Pain', that has attracted attention less for its merits
– it is efficient but not outstanding as verse – than for the light it seems
to throw on its author's inner life. Pain is seen as a sort of goddess with
the blessed power of obliterating grief, remorse and other spiritual
discomforts. This is an extreme view, and the poem certainly seems
to show first-hand knowledge of its subject. We are tempted to conclude, as at least one commentator has done, that only a deeply
unhappy man could have written it. But this conclusion should be
resisted. A poem is not a credo, not a considered statement of a settled
opinion (compare footnote, p. 94). Kipling did not really wish he
had toothache every time he was in low spirits, any more than he ran
his life on the principle that the female of the species is more deadly
than the male, or always went round muttering (let alone demon-
strating) that he travels the fastest who travels alone.

In some ways, the most interesting work of these last years is the
autobiographical *Something of Myself*, referred to earlier. The 'something' carries an ironical stress – 'but by no means everything'. None
of the emotional crises he underwent are discussed, and little is to be
learnt of his life in the domestic and social senses. As regards the part
he took in the literary world of his era, not much is said because there
is not much to say. Despite his immense celebrity, he remained an
isolated figure, a member of no group or alliance, adopting no attitude

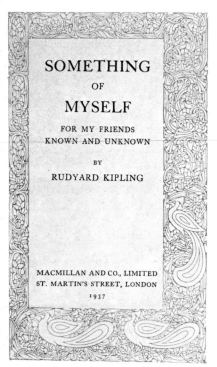

SOMETHING

OF

MYSELF

FOR MY FRIENDS
KNOWN AND UNKNOWN

BY

RUDYARD KIPLING

MACMILLAN AND CO., LIMITED
ST. MARTIN'S STREET, LONDON
1937

Title-page of *Something of Myself*,
published posthumously in 1937.

to any writer then living. He would not review books or otherwise pronounce on contemporaries.

On the positive side, *Something of Myself* gives some valuable and fascinating information about the United Services College, his 'seven years' hard' in India, and his stay in America. If some of this is the product of unconscious revision, what he felt when looking back tells us a great deal about him. With the unsurprising exceptions of life at Southsea and the bullying at the College, everything is seen tolerantly, much of it with a calm benevolence. His admission that he was fully capable of personal hatred testifies chiefly to unusual frankness and insight; it has been said that he was slow to forgive a slight, but at this stage any animosities seem long forgotten.

People who like that sort of thing – a large majority – will find here details of Kipling's working implements, his ink, his paper. We also learn of his trust in some tutelary creative force outside himself, something which most writers have confessed to, or will if challenged, under the name of inspiration, the Muse, instinct, one's little finger. Kipling responded to what he called his Daemon. He is slightly pompous on this subject, but very practical too. 'Take nothing for granted if you can check it . . . it encourages the Daemon' is sound advice.

His views on the cutting and compression of material are less sound. This is how he put them:

In an auspicious hour, read your final draft and consider faithfully every paragraph, sentence and word, blacking out where requisite. Let it lie to drain as long as possible. At the end of that time, re-read and you should find that it will bear a second shortening. Finally, read it aloud and at leisure. Maybe a shade more brushwork [i.e. cutting] will then indicate or impose itself. If not, praise Allah and let it go, and 'when thou hast done, repent not.' . . . I have had tales by me for three or five years which shortened themselves almost yearly.

And a bad thing too. I know some of those tales – 'Sea-Constables', 'Mrs Bathurst', 'As Easy as ABC' – and would rather have had them minus some of the 'brushwork'. The coyness of Kipling's language in the extract just given is a clue to how he regarded his craft: too much

Tibetan pen-case from Bateman's.

'Mr Rudyard Kipling turning out his "masterpieces"': the taint of journalism was attached to Kipling throughout his career.

as a craft, something too exclusively and self-absorbedly concerned with the craftsman and the finished product. *He* knew the full story in each case, so he would cut out the bits that bored him even if they contained necessary information, rather like a trendy film-editor of today. Kipling's indifference to public opinion of his work was admirable; indifference to that fundamental right of the reader, to be acquainted with what can be taken as the full facts, is a less fortunate trait. Though it showed only at intervals, Kipling stayed on the rebound from his journalist days for the rest of his life.

The last two pages of *Something of Myself* are all in the past tense: 'For my ink I demanded the blackest . . . I always kept certain gadgets on my work-table . . .'. This implied valediction is also a touchingly

Opposite, Poets' Corner, Westminster Abbey, 20 January 1936: not a single literary figure joined those who bore Kipling's ashes there.

At the funeral of Bonar Law, Westminster Abbey, 5 November 1927.

diffident appeal for pity. Kipling knew his end was near: three weeks off, as it proved.

Since 1915, Kipling had never for long been free of internal pain attributed to 'gastritis'. It was not until 1933, as his daughter writes, that duodenal ulcers were diagnosed, by which time an operation was thought inadvisable. Not long after his seventieth birthday he suffered a severe haemorrhage and was taken to Middlesex Hospital, where, on 18 January 1936, he died. He was cremated at Golder's Green and his ashes were laid in Poets' Corner in Westminster Abbey.

He had borne his illness with fortitude, not allowing it to diminish his essential good-nature. He was an affectionate man, especially towards children, who returned the feeling. His interest in people made him an excellent companion; his courtesy to strangers (as opposed to intruders) was often remarked. Apart from his attachment to Wolcott Balestier, and a less intense one to Rider Haggard (who died in 1925), he formed no very close friendships. The last dozen years of his life were overshadowed by that loneliness which had

always dogged him. Elsie's departure to get married in 1924 filled him with 'something like despair' – her phrase. Nevertheless, for a long time he was on the best of terms with a large number of people. Although his work, his politics and what he was felt in some general way to 'stand for' were often attacked (without ever bringing retaliation), no one said anything unpleasant about him personally, unless on occasion to notice what had been seen as his subservience to Carrie.

Unlike many writers, Kipling was good with his hands, always drawing, painting, manufacturing 'ancient' documents that were made to appear as authentic as possible, not only in orthography and calligraphy, but also in the appearance of the paper; all this for his own amusement. When amateur theatricals – a favourite diversion since his schooldays – were called for, he was the costume-jewellery man.

Food and drink appealed to him, at least until his ulcers began to give trouble. His American publisher, Frank Doubleday, records that, on arrival at Kipling's bedside in New York in 1899, his offers of help were met with the immediate request for a continuous supply of the best whisky available. (Andrew Carnegie had it and furnished it.) Kipling liked tobacco too, but again his health eventually demanded that he give up his beloved cigarettes in favour of a pipe.

He had no personal vanity, took no interest in clothes, and needed to be propelled by Carrie into going to his tailor. But he changed for dinner every night, because, after all, that was what you did, and what you did was probably the most sensible thing to do.

As early as 1900, Kipling's standing, secure enough with the reading public, began to be questioned by critics. This was partly, and quite naturally, because any new writer of obvious talent will seem to have something like infinite potential; only as he develops will his limitations declare themselves. But then there was the troublesome fact of his popularity: how could a serious writer be appreciated in music-halls? And the man who in India had been taken to be a hostile observer of the workings of the Empire was now emerging as its apologist, as the 'unofficial M.P. for British Possessions'.

That phrase was coined by Richard Le Gallienne, a poet and essayist born within a couple of weeks of Kipling. His *Rudyard Kipling: a criticism* (1900) set the tone for over a generation. The book is full of penetrating critical remarks, true and false predictions, and a mild liberal panic. *Barrack-Room Ballads* would remain Kipling's highest poetical achievement: well, yes. His prose style is 'the journalism of a man of genius, journalism vitalised by an imagination which usually reserves itself for higher forms of prose': only half the truth, but nicely put. What happens in a Kipling story is hard to remember afterwards – the telling is what counts: an exact comment on his weak narrative power.

'The Man That Is': cartoon of 1908.

'The Last of the Maffickers', a cartoon from the *Westminster Gazette* (July 1906), typifies the widely held but over-simplified view of him as an imperialist.

'Mr Kipling's general significance and influence' is viewed as dire in the extreme. 'Nothing if not reactionary', he glorifies war, and approval of violence creeps into supposedly impartial, documentary accounts: that last observation, variously rephrased, has gone on recurring as a major theme of Kipling's detractors to this day. After ever so many wringings, it still holds a drop of truth. Or, if 'approval' overstates the case, the reader can occasionally detect the lack of a sense of outrage when some sort of outrage would be in order. Le Gallienne finds autobiographical attitudes and emotions (sinister ones) in *The Light that Failed*, but he does not quote a very odd passage that seems to have escaped general attention on the part of Kipling-baiters. Dick Heldar is meditating on his approaching blindness.

There came to his mind the memory of a quaint scene in the Soudan. A soldier had been nearly hacked in two by a broad-bladed Arab spear. For one instant the man felt no pain. Looking down, he saw that his life-blood was going from him. The stupid bewilderment on his face was so intensely comic that both Dick and Torpenhow [Dick's fellow war-correspondent], still panting and unstrung from a fight for life, had roared with laughter, in which the man seemed as if he would join, but, as his lips parted in a sheepish grin, the agony of death came upon him, and he pitched grunting at their feet. Dick laughed again, remembering the horror. It seemed so exactly like his own case.

Really? Beyond doubt, that is just the sort of thing that happens on battlefields, and people will laugh at horrors when 'panting and unstrung', but afterwards. . . . It would not do to argue that when,

Opposite, Kipling had been in no doubt before the First World War of the dangers to peace, if we judge by this article from *The Daily Telegraph*, 17 March 1933.

say, Gloucester is blinded, Shakespeare is simply saying that this is no more than you might reasonably expect to happen when a British king makes an unwise decision. No, there is some want of heart in Kipling – in his work, that is to say – but it is what might be called patchy, not extensive. The man who could write 'Danny Deever' and 'Beyond the Pale', both of them pieces very much involving physical horror, did not suffer from callousness.

To finish with Le Gallienne: he was somewhere near the mark when he suggested that the, or a, reason for Kipling's popularity was that in him 'the Englishman as brute' and philistine had never had an admired writer on his side before: 'the thing was as true to life as the cinematograph of a prize-fight [in 1900! Could he have known that Kipling liked the movies?], and everyone said it was genius too.' Soften that 'brute' to 'not very literary or imaginative man', and we have an excellent explanation for Kipling's critical disrepute. To put it another way, as Le Gallienne does: 'For progressive thought there has been no such dangerous influence in England for many years', an unimprovably damaging and durable indictment in the eyes of a progressive intelligentsia.

So the case rested. It was reinforced by a vague but powerful feeling, among those looking back on the agonies of 1914–18, that what Kipling 'stood for' had helped to bring them about. (In fact, nobody had foreseen them more clearly or worked harder to avert them.) The tone of an obituary lecture delivered in the year of his death is hardly bold enough to be called defensive: he was a philistine, a tradesman, a tale-smith, perhaps forgivable in the light of his Southsea experience and slightly redeemed by the dependence of his poetry on work-rhythms.

In their different ways, Eliot and Orwell led the reaction in Kipling's favour. A poet who had once been the voice of England and tended to dislike her enemies might have something to be said for him in 1941, and Eliot's account of Kipling's virtues was both cogent and enthusiastic. Even so, puzzlement was aroused: could this be another of Mr Eliot's straightfaced jokes? Orwell's essay, coming from a man indisputably of the Left, must have been more upsetting. He had seen two vital facts: his experience of fascism in Spain and elsewhere had taught him that Kipling was not within a hundred miles of that position, and his experience of the Empire in the Burma Police, although it had made him a convinced anti-imperialist, had taught him that a man who identifies with the ruling power is not shedding but taking on responsibility; like it or not, the thing is there and somebody has to run it.

Quite soon afterwards, the Empire was no longer there and, as I have suggested, the man who had understood and described it, the only man to have done so, could be posthumously allowed to edge his

'The Englishman as brute'? Illustration from *Soldier Tales*, 1896.

Souvenirs of France.—V.

CLEMENCEAU'S VISION OF WAR

"Germans will Obey their Orders: We shall not Obey Even Ourselves"

By RUDYARD KIPLING

" Et ce n'est pas une vigilance d'un jour qui nous est demandée. Qui donc pourrait mesurer l'ampleur des oscillations auxquelles cette guerre a donné cours, ou prédire en quelles limites de temps pourra s'enclore l'evolution des conditions de vie mondiale successivement changées ? "

Georges Clemenceau.

FRENCHMEN remember (but we have forgotten) how the shadow of war darkened over Europe from 1907 onwards, when the watchword " World-Dominion or Downfall " was written, taught, prayed, preached, sculptured, set to music and legislated for as a Gospel, an end and a certainty.

Part of my winters I then used to spend at a " sports " hotel in Switzerland, frequented by German officers. On the day of their Kaiser's birthday they would dine—very well—and talk and sing of " The Day," with great clarity and many threats against all mankind.

THE FUROR TEUTONICUS

And not the officers alone. I recall, out of many, an interesting conversation with a most respectable Town Councillor of Hamburg. He laid down for me the minimum of his country's requirements from England. They included an "order" by the " English Parliament " to our " Colonies " to abolish all tariffs against his country, &c.

Failing this, the English were to beware of the " Furor Teutonicus " —as it might have been Ira Normanorum.

It was illuminating; it was as plain as the new railway siding at Hamburg—plain as their Press, or the way in which the German Colonies were armed and used as points of friction all over the world. That was before Agadir. Could France or England say they had not been warned ? . . .

(among critics and scholars) was in full swing, and today his standing is higher than ever before. Nevertheless, the argument is not ended: as John Gross wrote in 1972, Kipling 'remains a haunting, unsettling presence, with whom we still have to come to terms'.

What I have written is, I hope, partly a critical essay on Kipling, so to conclude I will confine myself to a few general statements.

Among the great volume of his work, a perhaps unexpectedly large amount can now be seen to be of the highest quality. The diverseness of his poetry alone is without parallel in our language, and, among the varied forms in which he excelled, the ones he invented himself pre-dominate. With all his breadth there went the gift of distilling a whole thought into a few memorable words. No modern writer has added more phrases to the language. As a travel writer he is unequalled, and has been very much undervalued. His one successful novel is a freak as well as a masterpiece, but he is clearly our best writer of short stories. Once again, his range is wide: the tragic, the comic, the satiric, the macabre, anecdote, fantasy, history, science fiction, children's tale. And he cuts deep. What if he never explored some emotions and some parts of experience? The ones he threw open are a more than sufficient compensation.

Above all, Kipling has power, sometimes the power to make us say, 'How dreadful!', more often the power that draws the pitifully rare response, 'I never thought of that.' He has it too in the sense of powerfulness, the ability to suggest in small compass that the events we are witnessing, or are about to witness, hold a unique importance. I can do no better than end with the opening, already mentioned, of ' "Love-o'-Women" ':

The horror, the confusion, and the separation of the murderer from his comrades were all over before I came. There remained only on the barrack-square the blood of man calling from the ground. The hot sun had dried it to a dusky gold-beater's-skin film, cracked lozenge-wise by the heat; and as the wind rose, each lozenge, rising a little, curled up at the edges as if it were a dumb tongue. Then a heavier gust blew all away down wind in grains of dark-coloured dust. It was too hot to stand in the sunshine before breakfast. The men were in barracks talking the matter over. A knot of soldiers' wives stood by one of the entrances to the married quarters, while inside a woman shrieked and raved with wicked filthy words.

SELECT BIBLIOGRAPHY

Charles Carrington, *Rudyard Kipling: his life and work* (London and New York, 1955; Harmondsworth, 1970): valuable not only for factual information but also for many interesting critical remarks. Essential to anybody interested in the subject as well as an outstanding book in its own right. Contains a fascinating Epilogue by Mrs George Bambridge (*née* Elsie Kipling).

Richard Le Gallienne, *Rudyard Kipling: a criticism* (London and New York, 1900): see pp. 110–12.

Edward Shanks, *Rudyard Kipling: a study in literature and political ideas* (London and New York, 1940; reprinted New York, 1971): thorough and fair-minded on the politics.

T. S. Eliot, ed., *A Choice of Kipling's Verse* (London and Toronto, 1941): includes long and important critical essay.

J. M. S. Tompkins, *The Art of Rudyard Kipling* (Lincoln, Nebraska, and London, 1959; 2nd ed. 1966).

Elliot L. Gilbert, ed., *Kipling and the Critics* (London and New York, 1965): reprints Orwell's essay (actually an extended review of Eliot, above) and some earlier critiques, also good contributions from C. S. Lewis, Steven Marcus and others.

Roger Lancelyn Green, *Kipling and the Children* (London, 1965): excellent on this essential part of Kipling and his work.

J. I. M. Stewart, *Rudyard Kipling* (London and New York, 1966): equal parts of biography and criticism. Hits many nails on the head.

Roger Lancelyn Green, ed., *Kipling: the critical heritage* (London and New York, 1971).

John Gross, ed., *Rudyard Kipling: the man, his work and his world* (London, 1972): illustrated. Many useful contributions, notably from Janet Adam Smith on the schooldays, N. C. Chaudhuri on *Kim*, Robert Conquest on the verse.

Charles Carrington, ed., *The Complete Barrack-Room Ballads of Rudyard Kipling* (London, 1974): the first complete collection, with helpful introduction and explanatory notes.

KIPLING'S PRINCIPAL WORKS

Departmental Ditties 1886
Plain Tales from the Hills 1888
From Sea to Sea 1889
The Light that Failed 1890, 1891*
Soldiers Three 1890
Wee Willie Winkie 1890
Life's Handicap 1891
The Naulahka (with Wolcott Balestier)
  1892
Barrack-Room Ballads and Other Verses
  1892
Many Inventions 1893
The Jungle Book 1894

* The 1891 version is the standard one.

The Second Jungle Book 1895
Captains Courageous 1897
The Day's Work 1898
Stalky & Co. 1899
Kim 1901
Just So Stories: for little children 1902
Traffics and Discoveries 1904
Puck of Pook's Hill 1906
Actions and Reactions 1909
Rewards and Fairies 1910
A Diversity of Creatures 1917
The Irish Guards in the Great War 1923
Debits and Credits 1926
Limits and Renewals 1932
*Something of Myself: for my friends known
  and unknown* 1937

LIST OF ILLUSTRATIONS

Frontispiece: Rudyard Kipling; pencil drawing by William Strang, ARA (1859–1921). *National Portrait Gallery, London.*

6 Caroline Kipling; painting by Sir Philip Burne-Jones. *Bateman's, Burwash, Sussex. Photo Eileen Tweedy.*

9 Rudyard Kipling; cartoon by Spy, published as the frontispiece of Kipling's *The Art of Fiction*, London 1926. *Courtesy of the Kipling Society and the Royal Commonwealth Society. Photo Eileen Tweedy.*

10 John Lockwood Kipling and Alice Macdonald Kipling. *Bateman's, Burwash, Sussex.*

11 Design for book-plate for Rudyard Kipling; pen and ink drawing by John Lockwood Kipling, 1909. *Bateman's, Burwash, Sussex. Photo Eileen Tweedy.*

12–13 Bombay harbour, *c.* 1870. *India Office Library and Records, London.*

14 Manati barber; photograph *c.* 1873, from *Archaeological Survey 52. India Office Library and Records, London.*

The Hajam or barber; drawing by John Lockwood Kipling, March 1872. *India Office Library and Records, London.*

15 Map of India, 1877; detail. *India Office Library and Records, London.*

Destruction caused by the Indian Mutiny at Lucknow; photograph by Felice Beato, 1857. *Victoria and Albert Museum, London.*

16 'What Impudence'; cartoon from *The Indian Punch*, 1 October 1863. *India Office Library and Records, London.*

17 Rudyard Kipling in his cot. *Bateman's, Burwash, Sussex.*

Announcement of the birth of Rudyard Kipling; published in

The Times of India, 2 January 1866. *India Office Library and Records, London.*

18 Rudyard Kipling, assisted by his servants. *Bateman's, Burwash, Sussex.*

19 'Ruddy's idea of heaven'; drawing by John Lockwood Kipling, 1868. *Bateman's, Burwash, Sussex.*

20 Cotton ground, Bombay, *c.* 1870. *India Office Library and Records, London.*

Borah Bazaar, Bombay, *c.* 1870. *India Office Library and Records, London.*

21 Rudyard Kipling, aged six. *Mansell Collection.*

22 Lorne Lodge, Southsea. *Courtesy Roger Lancelyn Green.*

The Grange, North End, Fulham, home of Sir Edward and Lady Burne-Jones. *Radio Times Hulton Picture Library.*

The Morris and Burne-Jones children in a garden, probably at the Grange; photograph by Emery Walker. *National Portrait Gallery, London.*

26 Astronomical globe with clock by Georg Roll and Johannes Reinhold, Augsburg, 1584. *Victoria and Albert Museum, London.*

Part of the last page of Charles Dickens's manuscript of *Edwin Drood*, 1870. *Victoria and Albert Museum, London.*

Manuscript of a poem by Rudyard Kipling. *Bateman's, Burwash, Sussex.*

27 Stanley Baldwin, aged nine. *Radio Times Hulton Picture Library.*

United Services Proprietary College, Westward Ho!, North Devon. *Mary Evans Picture Library.*

28 Kipling's room at Westward Ho!; drawing by G.C. Beresford (M'Turk). *Courtesy of the Kipling Society and the Royal Commonwealth Society. Photo Eileen Tweedy.*

Cormell Price. *Courtesy R.E. Harbord.*

29 Letter written by Rudyard Kipling on 9 March 1882; from W.M. Carpenter, *Kipling's College*, 1929. *Courtesy of the Kipling Society and the Royal Commonwealth Society. Photo Eileen Tweedy.*

30 Title-page: Q. *Horati Flacci, Carminum Librum Quintum*, translated by Rudyard Kipling and Charles Graves, Basil Blackwell, 1920. *Courtesy of the Kipling Society and the Royal Commonwealth Society. Photo Eileen Tweedy.*

32 Sir Edward Burne-Jones and William Morris in the garden at the Grange; photograph by Emery

Walker. *National Portrait Gallery, London.*

33 Frontispiece of *The Complete Stalky & Co. Courtesy of the Kipling Society and the Royal Commonwealth Society. Photo Eileen Tweedy.*

Rudyard Kipling as a schoolboy, *c.* 1882; from W.M. Carpenter, *Kipling's College, 1929. Courtesy of the Kipling Society and the Royal Commonwealth Society. Photo Eileen Tweedy.*

35 Rudyard Kipling, *c.* 1882. *Bateman's, Burwash, Sussex.*

36 Pan and Psyche; painting by Sir Edward Burne-Jones, 1872–74. *Fogg Art Museum, Harvard University. Grenville L. Winthrop Bequest.*

37 The gun 'Zam-Zammah' standing in front of the Lahore School of Art. *Mansell Collection.*

38 Page from the *Civil and Military Gazette,* 27 June 1885. *India Office Library and Records, London.*

39 The Lieutenant Governor of the Punjab's camel carriages outside Government House, Lahore, 1874. *India Office Library and Records, London.*

Lockwood Kipling's house in Lahore; drawing by John Lockwood Kipling. *Bateman's, Burwash, Sussex.*

40 Trix Kipling, Gattonside, Melrose, 1892. *Courtesy of the Kipling Society and the Royal Commonwealth Society. Photo Eileen Tweedy.*

41 Amateur theatricals in India, with Alice Kipling on the far right. *India Office Library and Records, London.*

43 View of Simla. *India Office Library and Records, London.*

Picnic given by the Viceroy's staff, Simla, 1891. *India Office Library and Records, London.*

44 Design for his own book-plate; terracotta plaque by John Lockwood Kipling. *Bateman's, Burwash, Sussex. Photo Eileen Tweedy.*

45 Front page of *The Pioneer,* 4 April 1887. *India Office Library and Records, London.*

46 Kipling's poem 'The Song of the Women'; published in *The Pioneer Mail,* April 1888. *India Office Library and Records, London.*

47 'Your potery very good, Sir; just coming proper length to-day'; from Jerome K. Jerome's *My First Book. Courtesy of the Kipling Society and the Royal Commonwealth Society. Photo Eileen Tweedy.*

48 Cover of *Under the Deodars*; published by Indian Railway Library (Lahore). *Courtesy of the Kipling Society and the Royal Commonwealth Society. Photo Eileen Tweedy.*

49 Cover of *The Phantom Rickshaw and other eerie tales*; published by Indian Railway Library (Lahore) and Sampson Low, Marston and Company (London). *Courtesy of the Kipling Society and the Royal Commonwealth Society. Photo Eileen Tweedy.*

50 The Town Hall and Mall, Simla; photograph *c.* 1890–1900. *India Office Library and Records, London.*

The loop, 'Agony Point', on the route of the Darjeeling Railway. *India Office Library and Records, London.*

51 Old Court House Street, Calcutta, looking north; photograph *c.* 1880–1890. *India Office Library and Records, London.*

Lead statue of an Indian deity, with a swastika carved on its head and a rose of peace held in its tusk. *Bateman's, Burwash, Sussex. Photo Eileen Tweedy.*

52 'On the Brain – Mr. Rudyard Kipling'; cartoon *c.* May 1892. *Courtesy of the Kipling Society and the Royal Commonwealth Society. Photo Eileen Tweedy.*

Title-page of *Indian Tales*, abridged and supplied with vocabulary by M. Lorie; published by the State Text-Book Publishing House of the People's Commissariat of Education of the R.S.F.S.R., Moscow 1940. *Courtesy of the Kipling Society and the Royal Commonwealth Society. Photo Eileen Tweedy.*

53 Proclamation of Queen Victoria as Empress of India, Delhi, January 1877. *India Office Library and Records, London.*

54 'William the Conqueror'; illustration from *The Day's Work* in *The Kipling Reader*, London 1908. *British Library, London.*

55 'Our Judge'; lithograph by W. O. Day in *Curry and Rice* by G. F. Atkinson, London 1911. *India Office Library and Records, London.*

56 Rudyard Kipling; photograph by 'Bourne and Shepherd of Simla, Calcutta, and Bombay'. *Bateman's, Burwash, Sussex.*

57 Roadside shrine in China; photograph from J. Thomson, *Illustrations of China and its People*, 1873.

58 Immigrants at Battery Park, New York, April 1896; photograph by Alice Austen. *Staten Island Historical Society.*

59 Kipling's house in Villiers Street, Strand, London. *Radio Times Hulton Picture Library.*

60 Cover of *Soldiers Three*; published by Indian Railway Library (Lahore), Sampson Low, Marston, Searle, & Rivington Limited (London), and Bromfield & Co. (New York). *Courtesy of the Kipling Society and the Royal Commonwealth Society. Photo Eileen Tweedy.*

61 Cover of *Wee Willie Winkie and other stories*; published by Indian Railway Library (Lahore) and Sampson Low, Marston & Company (London). *Courtesy of the Kipling Society and the Royal Commonwealth Society. Photo Eileen Tweedy.*

63 'The Man Who Would Be King'; terracotta plaque by John Lockwood Kipling. *Bateman's, Burwash, Sussex.*

65 Wolcott Balestier. *Houghton Library. By permission of the Harvard College Library.*

66 Colombo harbour, Ceylon (Sri Lanka), 1882. *Royal Commonwealth Society.*

67 Caroline Kipling; painting by Sir Philip Burne-Jones. *Bateman's, Burwash, Sussex. Photo Eileen Tweedy.*

68 Design for a book-plate for Elsie Kipling; pen and ink drawing by John Lockwood Kipling, 1908. *Bateman's, Burwash, Sussex.*

69 The Bliss Cottage, Brattleboro, Vermont, *c.* 1900. *Courtesy of Howard C. Rice, Jr.*

70 Main Street, Brattleboro, Vermont, *c.* 1890. *Courtesy of Howard C. Rice, Jr.*

Kipling in Main Street, Brattleboro, Vermont, 1893. *Courtesy of Howard C. Rice, Jr.*

71 Naulakha; photograph by H. C. Rice, Jr, December 1950. *Courtesy of Howard C. Rice, Jr.*

'Kipling at the wheelbarrow' at Naulakha, 1893; drawing from a clandestine photograph, 1893, published in *The Boston Globe*, 18 March 1894. *Courtesy of Howard C. Rice, Jr.*

72 View of Brattleboro from the Bliss Farm; photograph by Harold A. Barry, December 1973. *Courtesy of Howard C. Rice, Jr.*

73 Illustration from the first edition of *The Jungle Book*, 1894. *India Office Library and Records, London.*

74-75 Kipling's house at Rottingdean. *Mansell Collection.*

76 German efficiency in Africa; cartoon from *Jugend*, Munich 1896. *British Library, London.*

77 Kipling in Sweden to receive the Nobel Prize, 1907. *The Illustrated London News.*

78-79 Rudyard Kipling and Mark Twain (Samuel Clemens) receive honorary degrees in Oxford, 27 June 1907. *Bodleian Library, Oxford.*

80 Illustration from *Captains Courageous. Courtesy of the Kipling Society and the Royal Commonwealth Society. Photo Eileen Tweedy.*

81 The 'Depot', Brattleboro, Vermont, *c.* 1894. *Courtesy Howard C. Rice, Jr.*

82 'The Elephant's Child'; illustration drawn by Rudyard Kipling for the first edition of *Just So Stories*, 1902. *Courtesy of the Kipling Society and the Royal Commonwealth Society. Photo Eileen Tweedy.*

83 'Kim and the letter-writer'; illustration from a terracotta plaque made by John Lockwood Kipling for the first edition of *Kim*, 1901. *India Office Library and Records, London.*

84 Cecil Rhodes in 1897, on the site he chose for his grave. *Radio Times Hulton Picture Library.*

85 Title-page of *Ballads and Other Verses*, a pirated edition of Kipling's verse, published by Henry Altemus, Philadelphia *c.* 1897. *Courtesy of the Kipling Society and the Royal Commonwealth Society. Photo Eileen Tweedy.*

86 Josephine Kipling; photograph by A. D. Wyatt, *c.* 1895. *Courtesy of Howard C. Rice, Jr.*

87 Rudyard Kipling; painting by Sir Philip Burne-Jones, 1899. *National Portrait Gallery, London.*

88 The Royal Canadian Regiment and the 1st Gordon Highlanders fording the Modder River in February 1900 during the Boer War. *Public Archives of Canada.*

Kipling with other war correspondents at Glover's Island, *c.* 1900. *Radio Times Hulton Picture Library.*

89 Paardeberg, 1907; illustration from the Christmas 1900 edition of *Truth*. *Courtesy of the Kipling Society and the Royal Commonwealth Society. Photo Eileen Tweedy.*

90 Letter from Kipling to Strachey, written at Bateman's in 1902. *Formerly in the Beaverbrook Library, London. Photo Eileen Tweedy.*

91 Bateman's. *Photo National Trust.*

92 Bateman's: the front door, above which is carved the date of its construction. *Photo Eileen Tweedy.*

93 Bateman's: the entrance hall. *Photo Eileen Tweedy.*

Bateman's: Kipling's study. *Photo National Trust.*

94 Kitchener and Kipling; illustration from F. Carruthers Gould, *The Struwwelpeter Alphabet*, 1908. *Courtesy of the Kipling Society and the Royal Commonwealth Society. Photo Eileen Tweedy.*

96 The garden at Bateman's. *Photo A. F. Kersting.*

98 Kipling as a war correspondent in France. *Photo H. Roger Viollet.*

99 Kipling at a recruitment meeting in Southport, June 1915. *Bateman's, Burwash, Sussex.*

101 Sir Henry Rider Haggard, 1897. *Radio Times Hulton Picture Library.*

Rudyard and Carrie Kipling at the cemetery in Loos. *Photo H. Roger Viollet.*

102 'Brazilian Sketches'; published in *The Morning Post*, 9 December 1927. *Courtesy of the Kipling Society and the Royal Commonwealth Society. Photo Eileen Tweedy.*

104 Title-page of *Something of Myself*, London 1937. *Courtesy of the Kipling Society and the Royal Commonwealth Society. Photo Eileen Tweedy.*

105 Kipling at a garden party at the British Embassy, Paris, 1 July 1931. *Photo Associated Press.*

106 Tibetan iron pen-case. *Bateman's, Burwash, Sussex. Photo Eileen Tweedy.*

107 'Mr Rudyard Kipling turning out his "masterpieces"': cartoon from *The Windsor Magazine. Courtesy of the Kipling Society and the Royal Commonwealth Society. Photo Eileen Tweedy.*

108 The Kiplings at the funeral of Bonar Law, Westminster Abbey, 5 November 1927. *Photo Syndication International.*

109 Poets' Corner, Westminster Abbey, 20 January 1936. *Photo Associated Press.*

110 'The Man That Is'; cartoon by The Imp, March 1908. *Courtesy of the Kipling Society and the Royal Commonwealth Society. Photo Eileen Tweedy.*

111 'The Last of the Maffickers'; cartoon from the *Westminster Gazette*, 30 July 1906. *Courtesy of the Kipling Society and the Royal Commonwealth Society. Photo Eileen Tweedy.*

112 '"Shtrip bhoys," sez I'; illustration from *Soldier Tales*, 1896. *India Office Library and Records, London.*

113 'Souvenirs of France, V'; published by *The Daily Telegraph*, 17 March 1933. *Courtesy of the Kipling Society and the Royal Commonwealth Society. Photo Eileen Tweedy.*

115 Kipling; bronze portrait by Ginette Bingguely-Lejeune, 1936–37. *National Portrait Gallery, London.*

Page numbers in italics indicate illustrations

Aitken, Max 98, 99
Andersen, Hans 25
Austin, Alfred 77
Avery, Gillian 95

Baldwin, Alfred 12, 21
Baldwin, Louisa, *née* Macdonald 18,
  21, 24
Baldwin, Stanley 13, 27, *27*, 77, 103
Balestier, Beatty 68, 72
Balestier, Wolcott 64, 65, *65*, 66–69,
  69 n., 108
Beaverbrook, Lord *see* Aitken, Max
Beerbohm, Max 58
Buchanan, Robert 81
Buchman, Frank 101
Bunyan, John 25
Burne-Jones, (Sir) Edward 12, 21, 28,
  32, *32*, 36
Burne-Jones, Georgiana 21

Carnegie, Andrew 110
Carrington, Charles 66, 68, 103
Catullus 30
Chaucer, Geoffrey 104
Chaudhuri, Nirad C. 52, 83
Chesterton, G.K. 98
Clemenceau, Georges 94

Dickens, Charles 25, 27
Disney, Walt 73
Dobrée, Bonamy 97

Donne, John 31
Doubleday, Frank 110

Elgar, Edward 101
Eliot, T.S. 98, 112
Emerson, R.W. 31

Fielding, Henry 25
Fleming, Ian 81

Garrard, Florence 36, 59
George V, King 77, 101, 103
Gross, John 114

Haggard, (Sir) H. Rider 101, *101*, 108
Harte, Bret 31
Hitler, Adolf 103
Holloway, 'Uncle' Harry 21, 24
Holloway, 'Aunty' Rosa 21, 24, 25,
  36
Horace 30

James, Henry 66
James, William 66

Keats, John 95
Kipling, Alice, *née* Macdonald,
  Rudyard's mother *11*, 12–19, 21–25,
  28, 31, 41, *41*, 62, 65, 66

Kipling, Alice ('Trix'), later Mrs John Fleming, Rudyard's sister 18, 19, 21, 22, 25, 34, *40*, 41

Kipling, Caroline ('Carrie'), *née* Balestier, Rudyard's wife 6, 65, 66, 67, 68–72, 75, 84, 87, 90, 95, 98, 101, *101*, 110

Kipling, Elsie, later Mrs George Bambridge, Rudyard's daughter 68, 69, 75, 84, 87, 90, 95, 108, 110

Kipling, John, Rudyard's son 84, 90, 95, 98, 99

Kipling, John Lockwood, Rudyard's father 10–11, *11*, 12–19, 21, 28, 29, 31, 34, 37, 41, *44*, *44*, 66

Kipling, Josephine, Rudyard's daughter 69, 75, 84, 85, *86*, 87, 97

Kipling, (Joseph) Rudyard: physical characteristics 9; ancestry 10; parentage 10–14; birth 16; upbringing by Indian servants 16–19; character as child 18, 19; early experience of India 20; boarded out at Southsea 21–24; effect of Southsea years 24, 25; Epping Forest and Brompton Road 25, 27; insomnia 27; schooldays at United Services College 27–34; extent of education 30, 31; religion 31; other beliefs 32; first love 34, 36; sexual nature 36, 37; return to India 37; journalist at Lahore 37–42; life at Lahore and Simla 37–44; at Allahabad 44; at Calcutta 49; last days in India 51; effect of India on work 51, 52; political attitudes 52–55; journey through Far East 55, 57; USA 57, 58; settles in London 58; growing fame 59, 64; relations with Wolcott Balestier 64, 65, 68; meets Carrie 65; marriage 68; residence in Vermont 68–73; returns to England 75; refuses honours 77; inaccuracies 81; visits to South Africa 84–90; last visit to USA 85, 87; settles at Burwash, Sussex 90; 'Bateman's' (his house there) described 91, 92; impact of Great War 98, 99; post-war life 101, 103; possible melancholy of last years 104; methods of work 106, 107; final illness and death 108; character and habits 108, 110; critical reputation 110–14; merits summarized 114

Kitchener, Lord 95

Leacock, Stephen 94
Le Gallienne, Richard 110–12
Lermontov, Mikhail 33
Lloyd George, David 77
Longfellow, H.W. 31

Maugham, W. Somerset 62
Milner, (Sir) Alfred 84, 87
Morris, William 28, 32, *32*

Orwell, George 52, 76, 90, 112

Peacock, T.L. 31
Poe, E.A. 31
Poynter, (Sir) Edward 12, 21, 32
Price, Cormell 28, *28*, 29–31

Reade, Charles 84
Rhodes, Cecil 84, *87*, 88, 98

Shakespeare, William 64, 112
Sidney, Sylvia 98
Swinburne, A.C. 31

Taylor, Robert 98
Tennyson, Alfred (Lord) 77
Tompkins, J.M.S. 104
Twain, Mark 31, *78*

Verdi, Giuseppe 97
Vigny, Alfred de 33
Virgil 30

Waugh, Evelyn 57
Whitman, Walt 31

Yevtushenko, Yevgeny 52n.

INDEX OF REFERENCES TO KIPLING'S WORKS

Volumes are shown thus: *Debits and Credits*; stories thus: 'They';
poems thus: Danny Deever

Absent-Minded Beggar, The 89
Actions and Reactions 44, 95
'As Easy as ABC' 77, 106
'At the End of the Passage' 64

'Baa, Baa, Black Sheep' 22–25, 62, 97
Ballad of East and West, The, quoted
  54
Barrack-Room Ballads 59, 64, 68, 74,
  110
'Beauty Spots' 104
Beginnings, The 100
'Beyond the Pale' 48, 54, 64, 112
Boots 52 n.

Captains Courageous 69, 80
Children, The 100
'Conference of the Powers, A' 53
'Courting of Dinah Shadd, The' 64

Danny Deever 64, 112
'Dayspring Mishandled' 104
Day's Work, The 80
Debits and Credits 103
Departmental Ditties 44

'Eye of Allah, The' 104

'Fairy-Kist' 104
'Finest Story in the World, The' 73
'Flag of his Country, The' 34
For All We Have and Are 76
'Friendly Brook' 98
From Sea to Sea 44

'Habitation Enforced, An' 97, 98
'House Surgeon, The' 92, 95
Hymn to Physical Pain 104

'Judson and the Empire' 73
Jungle Books, The 55, 73, 73 n., 82
Just So Stories 82, 90

Kim 52 n., 83, 84, 98

Life's Handicap 64
Light that Failed, The 24, 36, 59, quoted
  111
Limits and Renewals 104
'Love-o'-Women' 74, quoted 114

M'Andrew's Hymn 75

'Madonna of the Trenches, A' 103
Mandalay 64
'Man Who Would Be King, The'
 62–64
Many Inventions 73
'Mark of the Beast, The' 64
Mary Gloster, The 75
'Mary Postgate' 100
'Matter of Fact, A' 73
Mesopotamia 100
Mine-Sweepers 100, 101
'Mrs Bathurst' 97, 106
'My Son's Wife' 98

Naulahka, The 65, 69 n.

'On Greenhow Hill' 64

Plain Tales from the Hills 44, 47, 48, 59,
 64
Puck of Pook's Hill 95, 97

Recessional 76
Rewards and Fairies 97

'Sea-Constables' 100, 106
Soldiers Three 59, 62
Something of Myself 20, 24, 104, quoted
 106, 107
Song in Storm, A 100
Song of the Banjo, The 74
Sons of Martha, The 97
Stalky & Co. 33, 34, 81, 82
Sussex 97, 98

'They' 97
Tommy, quoted 64
Traffics and Discoveries 95, 101

Wage-Slaves, The 97
'Walking Delegate, A' 73
Way through the Woods, The 97
Wee Willie Winkie 59, 62
White Man's Burden, The, quoted 54
'Wireless' 95
'Wish House, The' 103
'With the Night Mail' 97, 101
'Without Benefit of Clergy' 64

'·007' 81